Editor-in-Chief and Founder:
  Lyndon H. LaRouche, Jr.
Editorial Board: *Lyndon H. LaRouche, Jr. , Helga
  Zepp-LaRouche, Robert Ingraham, Tony
  Papert, Gerald Rose, Dennis Small, Jeffrey
  Steinberg, William Wertz*
Co-Editors: *Robert Ingraham, Tony Papert*
Technology: *Marsha Freeman*
Books: *Katherine Notley*
Ebooks: *Richard Burden*
Graphics: *Alan Yue*
Photos: *Stuart Lewis*
Circulation Manager: *Stanley Ezrol*

INTELLIGENCE DIRECTORS
Economics: *Marcia Merry Baker, Paul Gallagher*
History: *Anton Chaitkin*
Ibero-America: *Dennis Small*
Russia and Eastern Europe: *Rachel Douglas*
United States: *Debra Freeman*

INTERNATIONAL BUREAUS
Bogotá: *Miriam Redondo*
Berlin: *Rainer Apel*
Copenhagen: *Tom Gillesberg*
Lima: *Sara Madueño*
Melbourne: *Robert Barwick*
Mexico City: *Gerardo Castilleja Chávez*
New Delhi: *Ramtanu Maitra*
Paris: *Christine Bierre*
Stockholm: *Ulf Sandmark*
United Nations, N.Y.C.: *Leni Rubinstein*
Washington, D.C.: *William Jones*
Wiesbaden: *Göran Haglund*

ON THE WEB
e-mail: eirns@larouchepub.com
www.larouchepub.com
www.executiveintelligencereview.com
www.larouchepub.com/eiw
Webmaster: *John Sigerson*
Assistant Webmaster: *George Hollis*
Editor, Arabic-language edition: *Hussein Askary*

EIR (ISSN 0273-6314) *is published weekly
(50 issues), by EIR News Service, Inc.,
P.O. Box 17390, Washington, D.C. 20041-0390.
(703) 297-8434*

European Headquarters: E.I.R. GmbH, Postfach
Bahnstrasse 9a, D-65205, Wiesbaden, Germany
Tel: 49-611-73650
Homepage: http://www.eir.de
e-mail: info@eir.de
Director: Georg Neudecker

Montreal, Canada: 514-461-1557
eir@eircanada.ca

Denmark: EIR - Danmark, Sankt Knuds Vej 11,
basement left, DK-1903 Frederiksberg, Denmark.
Tel.: +45 35 43 60 40, Fax: +45 35 43 87 57. e-mail:
eirdk@hotmail.com.

Mexico City: EIR, Sor Juana Inés de la Cruz 242-2
Col. Agricultura C.P. 11360
Delegación M. Hidalgo, México D.F.
Tel. (5525) 5318-2301
eirmexico@gmail.com

Canada Post Publication Sales Agreement
#40683579

Postmaster: Send all address changes to *EIR*, P.O.
Box 17390, Washington, D.C. 20041-0390.

Signed articles in *EIR* represent the views of the authors,
and not necessarily those of the Editorial Board.

Enough!
Shut Down Mueller and the British Drive to War

Enough!
Call Congress and Your Senator and Tell Them To Shut Down Robert Mueller, Stop the British Drive to War

April 10—*In response to the British hoax being sold to President Trump for war in Syria and the dual operation by Robert Mueller, raiding the office of Trump's attorney to force the President to back Britain's war drive, the Lyndon LaRouche PAC issued the following mobilization statement on April, 10, 2018.* Executive Intelligence Review *endorses this call and asks its readers to join in this mobilization.*

We, the United States, are about to launch an attack on Syria and, possibly, the Russian troops therein, based on perfidious British lies; based on what may turn out to be history's final and blackest intelligence hoax, the one that eliminated the human race. At the same time, President Trump's personal lawyer's office was raided today, April 9, 2018, based on a referral from Special Counsel Robert Mueller. The issue apparently concerns allegations surrounding a years-old affair between the President and the lying and disgusting porn star Stormy Daniels. This is considered so serious by Mueller and our corrupt FBI, that the Sixth Amendment to the U.S. Constitution can be summarily tossed aside. These two outrageous events are completely related. Unless you rise up with us right now to stop it, this country is in grave, graver peril. The outright attempt to blackmail this President into the war he was elected to stop has been escalated beyond anyone's imagination.

In 2016, millions of Americans voted for Donald Trump because he said he would end useless, perpetual wars on behalf of an intellectually dead and financially bankrupt Anglo-American system, the imperium which dates to the immediate aftermath of World War II. That system, centered in Wall Street and the City of London, has ripped off the world, and destroyed the once-great U.S. economy, a fact which became completely evident to the sentient when the system crashed in 2008. Donald Trump sought better relations with China, now emerging as the world's most powerful economy, and Putin's Russia. Trump's determination to establish decent relations with Russia and China, and that determination alone, set into motion the hellish coup against the President, led by the British and those many useful idiots in our elites who are in their thrall.

That coup, whose manifesto was the fake "dirty dossier" on Donald Trump authored by MI6's Christopher Steele and paid for by Hillary Clinton, was on its last legs when Britain began its present offensive. Senators Charles Grassley and Lindsay Graham had referred Christopher Steele to the United States Department of Justice for criminal prosecution, and patriots in Congress were pursuing a genuine effort to identify and prosecute those responsible for the coup against our President.

Then, on March 4, 2018, a Russian who spied for Britain, Sergei Skripal, and his daughter were allegedly poisoned in Salisbury, England. Skripal runs in the same British espionage circles associated with Christopher Steele. Prime Minister Theresa May immediately pronounced to the world that Russia was behind the attack, but has never ever produced any proof for any of her bellicose statements. President Trump was bumrushed by his traitorous advisors, including H.R. McMaster, who throughout his military career was a captive of Britain's International Institute of Strategic Affairs, into supporting Britain's completely unfounded claims.

The message to the President from our traitors is clear: join us in the march to war and maybe, maybe, we will let up with the coup.

Ultimately, Britain's own chemical weapons experts at Porton Down refused to say that the agent used on the Skripals was manufactured in Russia, despite the evidence-free claims of Theresa May and her insane Foreign Minister, Boris Johnson. Obvious doubts had already been voiced by several European countries which abstained from Britain's call to war. Among the facts considered: The deadly nerve agent described by May would have immediately killed Skripal and his daughter. Yet, both are alive and out of critical condition. Accounts of where it was administered have varied; most recently it was said to have been smeared on the front door handle of Skripal's home. Yet, Skripal somehow managed to leave the house for some hours, walking around the village, drinking and eating at restaurants until he suddenly fell ill. The formula for the alleged poison had been widely published by its Russian inventor, a dissident now living in the United States. Now, with that hoax disintegrating, we are told that the Skripals and all possible evidence in the case are being disappeared. According to the British press, they will be put in a CIA Witness Protection Program. Their house and every alleged crime scene involved in this hoax are being bull-dozed and destroyed. No possibility of an actual investigation of this hoax is to be left open.

Despite voicing support for Theresa May, Donald Trump still sought to make good on his promise to the American people. He congratulated Putin on his election and invited him to the White House for early talks, citing the escalating and dangerous arms race between the United States and Russia. The British and their American friends completely lost it in response. They decided a hammer needed to be dropped on this President who now was even talking of pulling American troops out of Syria and rebuilding the United States.

Enter a second British-authored poisoning hoax, this one in Syria, where the Russians, Iranians, and Syrians not only assisted in the defeat of Isis, but were mopping up the last remnants of remaining jihadis, such as Jayish Al-Islam, a rebranded Salafist Jihadi group controlled by the Saudis, and the Al-Nusra front or Al-Qaeda. The final military operations consolidating victory were concluded in the last days in Ghouta, a suburb of Damascus. Having achieved victory, under the narrative our war-mongering media would have us believe, Assad launched a chemical weapons attack to celebrate that victory, knowing he would bring down holy hell upon himself from the West.

The pictures of dying children which President Trump reacted to so emotionally a year ago, when he launched missile strikes on Syria, have been presented to him again. There is every reason to believe they are fake. Russia and Syria had been warning about just such a false-flag attack involving chlorine gas for over a month as they closed in on victory in Gouta. The only information claiming such an attack occurred is coming from the White Helmets, an aid organization founded by the British, implicated as being militarily involved with Al-Qaeda, and deeply implicated in past hoaxes concerning Assad's alleged use of chemical weapons. Sy Hersh fully documented this story in the *London Review of Books,* concerning the fake news that Assad used Sarin in August of 2013. MIT's Ted Postol and others have demonstrated that the alleged sarin attack to which President Trump responded militarily one year ago, was also a British fake. See, Robert Parry, https://consortiumnews.com/2017/09/07/a-new-hole-in-syria-sarin-certainty/ and James Carden, https://www.thenation.com/article/the-chemical-weapons-attack-in-syria-is-there-a-place-for-skepticism/.

The White Helmets are jointly funded by British and American intelligence components dedicated to regime-change in Syria. They have received millions upon millions of dollars for this purpose. They are critical components of the interventionist and regime-change foreign policy Donald Trump was elected to eradicate.

In 2013, when Obama threatened war with Russia over Syria, the American people intervened, raised the roof of Congress, and stopped it. This is what is needed now. Russia sees an unrelenting information warfare offensive coming from the British and their dupes in the U.S. They correctly see this as the first steps toward war. We need to reverse this starting right now. Call your Congressional Representative or Senator, tell them to Stop the drive to war and Shut down Robert Mueller, Now. The Capitol Switchboard is 202-224-3121.

Skripal Gambit Blows Up in May's Face, Trump Moves Ahead on Diplomatic Fronts

by Harley Schlanger

April 6—If the intent of the absurd charges flung at Russian President Putin—by Britain's Prime Minister Theresa May and her Foreign Minister Boris Johnson—was to drive a wedge between U.S. President Trump and Russian President Putin, it has failed miserably. May not only accused Putin's intelligence operatives of poisoning former Russian spy and British double agent Sergey Skripal and his daughter Yulia, but demanded that governments accept her accusations and join Britain in imposing sharp penalties against Russia. While the United States, fourteen EU nations, and six other governments went along with May, expelling more than 130 Russian diplomats, the British were not pleased, as many governments, including some which did expel Russian diplomats, expressed doubts about the lack of evidence to prove the charges, and President Trump repeatedly refused to blame Putin, though his government did expel diplomats.

When it was subsequently announced that the Trump administration will allow the Russians expelled fr om the United States to be replaced by others, and that Russia would reciprocate, demonstrating that the expulsions were at best a token gesture, it added to the British sense that they were being betrayed by Trump.

Doubts about May's and Johnson's charges proved to be prophetic, with the April 3 announcement by Gary Aitkenhead, Chief Executive of the Defence Science and Technology Laboratory (DSTL), the British chemical warfare research center at the Porton Down science park, that the investigating team was unable to determine where the chemical agent used against the Skripals came from, and specifically, that they could not prove it came from Russia. The *London Times* was forced to admit that Aitkenhead's report "risks undermining the international coalition against Moscow."

The *Guardian*, which had been one of the more aggressive media outlets in its attacks on Moscow (and in promoting the Russiagate narrative against Trump and Putin), complained that UK officials were "thrown on the defensive" by Aitkenhead's report, while British opposition leader Jeremy Corbyn went even further, essentially accusing Johnson of lying. He said that Johnson has "egg on his face," and has "serious questions to answer," given that Johnson told German television— as well as anyone else who would listen—that Porton Down had assured him "categorically" that Russia was the source of the Novichok chemical agent deployed against the Skripals. Corbyn said that Johnson "seems to have completely exceeded the information he had been given, and told the world, in categorical terms what he believed had happened, and it's not backed up by the evidence he claimed to have gotten from Porton Down."

That the Brits lied, in pursuit of an anti-Putin, anti-Trump agenda, is no surprise to readers of *EIR*, and to supporters of the LaRouche movement, which has long documented the sordid history of war provocations coming from the defenders of the British empire. In the last fifteen years, the British government and its intelligence officials have been caught in repeated lies to promote regime-change wars, beginning with Tony Blair's lying dossier alleging that Iraq's President Saddam Hussein possessed weapons of mass destruction that could land in London within 45 minutes of being launched. That dossier, produced under the direction of MI6 head Sir Richard Dearlove, was used by the Bush-Cheney administration to justify the 2003 invasion and destruction of Iraq, which resulted in more than a million deaths and the launching of ISIS. The same networks lied that Syrian President Assad had used chemical weapons against his own people, while they and their Obama administration allies were busy arming the "rebels" in Syria, and covering up *their* use of chemical weapons.

The same Dearlove has been exposed as playing a key role in the distribution of the fraudulent "dodgy dossier" produced by one of his protégés, "ex"-MI6 agent Christopher Steele, which has been at the center of regime-change operations against U.S. President Trump. It should be noted that there is a Steele connection to the Skripal case, as he was a key operative on the Russia Desk of MI6 when Skripal was functioning as a double agent. Skripal's recruiter, former MI6 agent Pablo Miller, according to the *Telegraph*, was working then for Steele's firm, Orbis Business Intelligence, leading to speculation that perhaps Skripal may have been involved in some way in producing the Steele dossier, and that's why he was targeted, not by the Russians, but by the British!

Trump's Diplomatic Agenda

As the British effort to use the Skripal affair was unfolding, with demands that Russia be punished, President Trump made a high-profile phone call to Putin on March 21, to congratulate him on his re-election. The U.S. media highlighted the story that Trump aides had specifically advised him *not* to congratulate Putin, and demanded that press secretary Sarah Sanders explain why Trump did not question Putin about Putin's alleged involvement in poisoning Skripal. What Sanders reported shocked the anti-Trumpers in the media: Not only had Trump not confronted Putin, but he invited him to meet in the "not-distant future."

In a campaign-style rally several days later in Ohio, Trump reiterated his oft-stated position that he believes it is better to have good relations with Russia. He said it again on April 3, in a press appearance with the presidents of three Baltic states saying, "we want to be able to get along with Russia. Getting along with Russia is a good thing, not a bad thing." He said this while flanked by presidents who have been warning that their countries might be targets of "Russian aggression"!

At the same time, Trump followed up his announcement, from earlier in the week, that he intends to remove all U.S. troops from Syria. "I want to get out," he said. "I want to bring our troops back home." The "primary mission" of our presence in Syria was the defeat of the Islamic State, which he said is "almost completed." Left unsaid by the President, but obvious to all, is that the main work done to defeat ISIS was done by the forces of the Syrian government, backed primarily by Russia.

Under Trump, U.S. military forces operating against ISIS have engaged in regular consultation with the Russians. His announcement that it is time to pull U.S. troops out of Syria completely conforms with his campaign pledge that, under his presidency, U.S. soldiers would not die in regime-change wars and U.S. taxpayers would not pay trillions of dollars to interfere in the sovereign affairs of other nations. This pledge was in direct opposition to what his opponent, Hillary Clinton, said. Clinton said she would enforce "no-fly zones" in Syria, which could have led to military conflict with Russian forces there. It is one of the reasons that the "Deep State"—the pro-war grouping of U.S. intelligence operatives closely aligned with the British—has been so feverishly engaged in trying to remove Trump. Among the top officials deployed against Trump has been Obama's national security team, including former CIA Director John Brennan, former FBI Director James Comey, former Director of National Security and Russophobe James Clapper, and former President Barack Obama himself. All are now being investigated, by Congress and the Justice Department, for their role in coordinating the attacks on the Trump presidency with Steele and British intelligence.

In addition to his plan to meet soon with Putin, Trump is involved in ongoing discussions on trade and economic relations with China's President Xi Jinping, as well as on the prospects for an upcoming summit with North Korea's Kim Jong-un, and he will meet soon with Japanese Prime Minister Shinzo Abe.

This schedule makes clear that British-directed operations against him, such as the Russiagate investigation and the Skripal case, have not deterred Trump from his stated intent to reverse the paradigm of the Bush and Obama years, when the United States functioned, in full collaboration with the Brits, as though it were the world's only power, capable of dictating terms to all, and carrying out provocations against Russia and China.

EIR Contents

www.larouchepub.com   Volume 45, Number 15, April 13, 2018

Cover This Week

UK Prime Minister Theresa May (left) and Foreign Secretary Boris Johnson.

ENOUGH! SHUT DOWN MUELLER AND THE BRITISH DRIVE TO WAR

2 LAROUCHE PAC EMERGENCY STATEMENT
Enough! Call Congress and Your Senator and Tell Them To Shut Down Robert Mueller, Stop the British Drive to War

4 Skripal Gambit Blows Up in May's Face, Trump Moves Ahead on Diplomatic Fronts
by Harley Schlanger

I. The Strategy for Humanity

7 ZEPP-LAROUCHE WEBCAST
The New Silk Road Is Shaping Strategic Affairs

14 'The Campaign To Win the Future' Means Ending the Party Politics of the Past
by Susan Kokinda

17 SCHILLER INSTITUTE REPORT
Houston Mobilizes for Mankind's Shared Future
by Brian Lantz

21 CHINA REPORT
The Silk Road Reaches Africa

24 Who Is Out To Control Africa's Mining Sector?

25 The Eurasia Canal
by Dean Andromidas

II. What Stands in the Way

30 A DIALOGUE OF THREE PRESIDENCIES
Bending the Arc of the Moral Universe Toward Justice
by Helga Zepp-LaRouche

39 SOUTH AFRICAN GREETINGS TO NYC SCHILLER INSTITUTE CONFERENCE
There Can Be No Justice Through Violence

III. Lyndon LaRouche: May 8, 2014

41 EXTENDED REMARKS & FACTS:
Economists Who Were Usually Stupid
by Lyndon H. LaRouche, Jr.

ZEPP-LAROUCHE WEBCAST

The New Silk Road Is Shaping Strategic Affairs

This is the edited transcript of the April 5, 2018 Schiller Institute New Paradigm webcast, an interview with the founder of the Schiller Institutes, Helga Zepp-LaRouche. She was interviewed by Harley Schlanger. A video of the webcast is available.

Harley Schlanger: Hello, I'm Harley Schlanger from the Schiller Institute. Welcome to this week's Schiller Institute webcast for April 5, 2018, featuring our founder Helga Zepp-LaRouche.

In the last couple of weeks, Helga has spoken about the potential for a backfire as a result of the Skripal affair that British Prime Minister Theresa May and her somewhat unhinged Foreign Secretary, Boris Johnson, have been using as a way of attacking both Russia and the United States. We've seen this play out in a very big way in the last couple of days. The fact that the British have come out in their own name, and in the name of their intelligence services and their government, to attack Russia, has in fact, "put egg on their faces," as some

have said. So, Helga, why don't you catch us up on what's happened in the last days? Because this is quite significant, in terms of shaping the strategic relationships.

Helga Zepp-LaRouche: This is extremely serious. The group of nations, which moved in unprincipled solidarity with May and Johnson, need to reflect on what has actually happened. Look at some of the recent developments: Gary Aitkenhead, the Chief Executive of the Defence Science and Technology Laboratory at Porton Down, said in an interview, that the lab could not find any proof that the origin of this nerve agent was Russia; the lab did establish that it was Novichok, or belonged to the group of Novichoks, but could not definitely say that it came from Russia.

This has led to quite a series of events. One was that the British Foreign Office removed the tweet in which it had earlier insisted that there was no doubt that the origin of the poison was Russia, and I think it

UK Foreign Secretary Boris Johnson.

UK Prime Minister Theresa May

even mentioned that the scientists of the Porton Down lab had said so. So, they were obliged to remove the tweet, because that also constitutes evidence that Boris Johnson was lying, because he had said that he had heard from the scientists that there was irrefutable proof that this came from Russia. That's the first thing.

Then *The Times* of London had a comment saying that the statement by Aitkenhead threatens to collapse the international coalition against Russia. Well, that's indeed the case, because now everyone is reviewing the case. For example, at a press conference held by the German government shortly after Aitkenhead's statement, journalists asked if the German government had changed its perspective. The answer was no. This clearly demonstrates the nature of the stranglehold on the minds of these people. They are in the grip of the British empire.

This operation is now clearly backfiring. The role of the British government, and the British empire, is completely exposed. They, however, are not stopping their confrontation with Russia. Some of the Russian response can be heard from speakers at the Seventh Moscow Conference on International Security, now taking place in Moscow. Sergei Naryshkin, for example, who is the head of Russia's Foreign Intelligence Service said that this is as serious as the Cuban Missile Crisis in 1962. Others said that this time these idiots have gone way over the line, and that is clearly the case. There is, fortunately, a wide array of people who are saying, look, we cannot continue this way; we have to resume a dialogue with Russia; we have to go back to straighten out relations.

Despite the fact that the United States expelled 60 Russian diplomats, which is clearly part of Britain's escalation, President Trump himself did not at any point use the Skripal incident to attack Russia as the perpetrator; this stands out clearly. People, who are always totally freaked out about Trump, should seriously review the truth of the matter and ask themselves if their perspective and their approach are correct. It is not, for the most part, Trump who is going for confrontation. The actual warmongers turn out to be people who can't even walk straight, claiming that they are so heavily burdened with their responsibilities to enforce "democracy and human rights." People need to think this through.

If you consider the procedures that NATO, part of the European Union, and the German and French governments have taken, all immediately jumping on Brit-

The George W. Bush Presidential Library
Above: UK Prime Minister Tony Blair (left) at a meeting meeting with President George W. Bush in 2002 to pressure Bush to launch the war against Iraq. Left: Dr. David Kelly, who was "suicided" in 2003.

ain's evidence-free condemnation of Russia, these actions constitute a blow to the whole Western system. These actions are wreaking great damage to the Western system by allowing the condemnation to come first, by having Russia declared guilty, before any establishment of scientific fact, by claiming that perhaps evidence will surface sometime down the road, or maybe not. Any nation that plays with these things lightly is contributing to discrediting itself, which is not a good thing.

Schlanger: Minimally, we could say this is a rush to judgment, but more importantly, this is part of an established pattern of British intelligence. We've seen it before with the repeated charges, without evidence: that the Assad government was using chemical weapons against its own people, and of course, the famous case even earlier of Tony Blair's story about Iraq's possession of weapons of mass destruction, which turned out to be another fabrication of the highest levels of British intelligence.

But there's another aspect of this which I think you may want to comment on, which is the case of David Kelly, because this also hits at home, where there was opposition from within the scientific community in the United Kingdom against the actions of the government and the intelligence community.

Zepp-LaRouche: This is clearly a pattern. Before the statement by the head of the Porton Down lab came out, the former British ambassador to Uzbekistan, Craig Murray, had said that he had it from high-level sources in the intelligence community or the science community, that the British scientists could not produce the evidence—and they didn't. At the time of the Iraq War, David Kelly, UN weapons inspector and Porton Down division head, had blown the whistle, reporting that there were no weapons of mass destruction, for which truth-telling he met with an early death under extremely dubious circumstances, which was said to be a suicide, but nobody really believes that.

I think this is quite something. The Iraq war was based on lies. Willy Wimmer, the former vice president of the Organization for Security and Co-operation in Europe (OSCE) and former state secretary to the German Federal Minister of Defense, pointed to the fact that the Iraq War, after all, has caused hundreds of thousands of deaths in Europe, in the Middle East, and in North Africa. The Chilcot Commission, which from our standpoint was somewhat a cover-up, did, nevertheless, point to the fact that Tony Blair had willfully, intentionally exaggerated the danger coming from Iraq and Saddam Hussein at the time. Bush's Secretary of State, Colin Powell, used the MI6 "dodgy dossier" on Iraq's alleged "weapons of mass destruction" to argue before the UN Security Council for the United States to join in the Iraq War.

Governments have launched these wars in which, looking at them in their totality, millions of lives have been lost. There has been no accountability, it just goes by. The people, who claim to be defenders of human rights and democracy, are the same people who make these interventions into sovereign countries, which have had such horrible results. This is complete hypocrisy and duplicity. And then they act self-righteous, pre-

Carl-Theodor-Molinari-Stiftung
Willy Wimmer

UN/Mark Garten
Colin Powell

tending they are the good ones, and the Russians and the Chinese are the bad ones.

I think we need to review all of this, because it cannot be allowed to continue. It's very dangerous to world peace.

Schlanger: Another aspect of this is that it was a major feature of President Trump's election campaign in 2016, in which he, at a very important debate in South Carolina, openly accused George W. Bush of lying to create the Iraq War, and he said that his administration would oppose these kinds of wars.

This week the President announced that he's preparing to remove U.S. troops from Syria, despite demands from some in the military and the CIA, that the United States remain in Syria.

This is a fairly significant departure from the standard Bush/Obama policy of pursuing these wars, isn't it?

Zepp-LaRouche: Yes, Trump is clearly sticking to his campaign stances despite the fact that certain representatives of the U.S. military and related circles are saying, "No, no, we still have a lot of fighting to do against ISIS." He has promised to stop the interventionist wars, and I think he is going very far to do so. Especially, if you consider that in this middle of this whole hysteria, he telephoned President Putin and reiterated that he wants to have a summit with him in the near future. President Trump stated that having a good relationship with Russia "is a good thing and not a bad thing," in the midst of his meetings with the presidents of Estonia, Latvia, and Lithuania, the three Baltic countries that are extremely anti-Russian.

Those who have blindly accepted the slanders against Trump, Putin, and Xi should consider that these slanders originate from the same circles—the neo-con, neo-liberal geopolitical factions—that recognize that their system is in really bad shape and will stop at nothing to save it, as is evident in the recent Skripal affair.

Schlanger: You mentioned the Moscow International Security Conference. Clearly, there's a discussion going on there, about something that your husband Lyndon LaRouche brought up many, many years ago, and that you've been calling for, which is the establishment of a new security architecture. How is this proceeding in Moscow? Do you have some reports on what the discussion process has been there?

Zepp-LaRouche: It's an extremely important event. There are 95 countries represented, 840 guests,

Russian President Vladimir Putin (left) and Turkish President Recep Tayyip Erdogan.

and 700 media. This alone speaks to the fact that Russia is very far from being isolated, as some in the West are trying to portray.

The discussions were very focussed on the need to have an international alliance to combat terrorism. There was a warning by the Director of the FSB, that there are signs that ISIS and al-Qaeda are merging. He said this means you will have sleepers and cells in every country around the globe, and the only way you can defend against that, is to work together internationally.

Another very important aspect of this conference, is that the Defense Minister of China went to this conference and made a statement that his attendance was meant as a signal to the West that the Russian and the Chinese military are in an extremely close strategic partnership.

There were many warnings that the present confrontation is approaching the danger level of the Cuban Missile Crisis, so people are extremely attuned to what is coming from the British and their allies. On the other hand, it also shows who is talking in favor of international solidarity and cooperation to address the real dangers of the world. Clearly Russia, China, and the other countries participating in this conference, not the British led Western group, are addressing the real dangers in the world.

And again, this is something people should reflect on, rather than believing the propaganda. If you read the German tabloid *Bildzeitung* this morning, on page 2, it has a photo montage of Putin, Erdogan, and Rouhani, and it labels them as an "axis of evil." This is ridiculous!

These three countries—Russia, Turkey, and Iran—have collaborated to bring about a solution to the terrible crisis in Syria, and this *is* a very good thing. Not all aspects of the policies of these countries,— there are the unresolved tensions between the Kurds and Erdogan, between Turkey and Greece, so not everything is perfect.

In the larger picture, look at the fact that the misery of the Syrian people, who have suffered through war for seven years, is being positively addressed and alleviated precisely because of the intervention of these three countries, and do not forget the cooperation between the United States and Russian military under the leadership of Trump and Putin. Don't just fall for the propaganda spread by such media coverage. There are many people who have suffered great losses, of their livelihoods, their happiness, and even their lives as a result of the British empire's geopolitical policies For the Syrian people, this help is a very good thing.

Schlanger: Especially, this should have meaning for people in Europe, because in 2015-2016, there was the explosion of the refugee crisis, and with all the hand-wringing and crocodile tears that were shed, nothing was done to support the Russian intervention to stop the war in Syria. The fact that the Russian, Iranian, and Turkish governments were meeting to discuss this, is something that should be welcomed, as opposed to being a source for criticism.

On Russia-Turkey cooperation, there was another aspect to it, because when these problems are dealt with in the real world, there's always an economic element.

Putin and Turkish President Erdogan recently reached an agreement to move ahead with nuclear energy development. This is part of the broader package of the New Silk Road and economic cooperation that you've been talking about, isn't it?

Zepp-LaRouche: Yes. The remarks of President Putin, who was at the opening ceremony of this Akkuyu nuclear plant, were meant to emphasize the extreme importance of nuclear energy, giving a country cheap and secure energy, and leading to an increase in the productivity of its entire economy; which is absolutely the case. There are many, many nuclear energy projects under construction with the help of Russia, China, and India—in Africa, in Latin America, and in Asia.

Soon, countries such as Germany will be the only ones not having nuclear energy, and if they keep to this course, these countries will be sidelined to the disadvantage of their own people. This is something we must change.

Schlanger: Another story getting a lot of coverage internationally is that the discussions and negotiations under way between the United States and China on tariff policy are nothing but a trade war. I think it's being covered by the media as a way of trying to drum up war. There is danger in this, as the Chinese have pointed out. I think it's important to hear your perspective. There are problems in the U.S.-China relationship including the huge trade imbalance, but it's not just a trade war, there is a much broader discussion under way. How do you see this evolving, from what you've seen recently?

Zepp-LaRouche: There are negotiations going on, and it may not necessarily come to the execution of these tariffs, which both sides have now drawn up, ranging up to $60 billion in products. Chinese Prime Minister Li Keqiang has pointed out that there is another way to overcome the trade imbalance, namely by increasing trade, especially by investments in joint ventures in third countries—that there are many ways to get rid of this trade imbalance.

There is renewed discussion of something which we brought in early on, namely, the possibility of Chinese investments in infrastructure in the United States. That would also be a way to completely change the dynamic. Chinese investment in American infrastructure would create many, many productive jobs for Americans; it would create the infrastructure necessary as a precondition for a real industrial revolution: for the building of new cities, science cities, connecting all American cities with fast train systems.

There are so many ways of changing the dynamic for the better. I'm convinced that China has this in mind. There was a program recently on the Chinese TV channel CGTN, proposing exactly that idea: that there should be a dialogue on infrastructure. A Trump supporter made such a proposal recently. Such a discussion has begun. President Xi Jinping will be giving a very important speech at the Boao Forum for Asia, known to some as the "Asian Davos," which will start on April 8. He is expected to make quite a significant, major speech on the continuation of international reforms, and opening up. You can expect something important to come from there.

The Chinese are also extremely aware of the fact that we are sitting on a powder keg in terms of the financial system. Xi Jinping has defined three priorities: One, to overcome the risks of the financial system; two, to alleviate poverty; and three, to get rid of air pollution. So I think the Chinese are very much aware of the dangers of the current Western financial system. There were several articles recently warning that the outbreak of a new 2008 crisis could happen at any moment. One of the many new aspects being looked at is the difference between the LIBOR rate and the Fed rate. That was the early sign of the start of the 2008 crisis.

So that requires an acceleration of the discussion which we and our colleagues in the United States and in Europe have initiated, to implement the Four Laws of Lyndon LaRouche: Glass-Steagall, a national bank, a credit system, and cooperation of the Western countries with the financial systems of the New Silk Road, the AIIB, and the New Silk Road Fund. All of these things need to be urgently discussed because of the very great and present danger of a financial crash. Some people are even speculating that the same people taking these provocative actions against Russia, could also deliberately trigger such a financial crash, to pull the rug out from under President Trump and bring the neo-cons back, getting rid of Trump by blaming the crash on him.

To anyone who thinks this is a conspiracy theory, or totally over the top, I strongly suggest looking again at the Skripal case. Learn the lesson from that. Learn how things can be manipulated and orchestrated.

The urgency is to quickly draw the proper lesson from all of this, and end this system of looting, which only serves the very few, very rich; it's destroying the middle class; it's making the poor, poorer. We need a return to Hamiltonian economics. This is the basis of the Chinese economic miracle, as I have said many times.

Chinese State Councilor and Foreign Minister Wang Yi and Swiss Federal Councillor and Foreign Minister Ignazio Cassis hold the first round of foreign ministerial strategic talks between the two countries in Beijing, April 3, 2018.

The Chinese economic miracle, or Chinese economic model, is much, much closer to the economic policies of the young republic of the United States than many think. It's no coincidence that the distinction which Friedrich List, for example, made between the American System and the British System, is exactly what is playing out today, and that's why we **clearly** need a return to the American System of economy.

Schlanger: It's also important to keep in mind that President Trump has repeatedly referred to his great friendship with Xi Jinping, and the strategic importance of a U.S.-China relationship is also clear when it comes to collaboration in bringing a peaceful solution to the Korean Peninsula. There's a lot of diplomacy coming up: The Trump-Putin meeting; the Trump meeting with Prime Minister Abe of Japan; and also his coming meeting with Kim Jong-un. So there's a lot more at stake here than just reducing the U.S. trade imbalance.

Just to go back to one final note on the Belt and Road Initiative: I'm sure you took note of the importance of the recent visit of the delegation from the Swiss government to China, and also the very large delegation heading to China from Austria. Maybe there's a lesson here for Germany?

Zepp-LaRouche: Well, one would hope so. I am very happy that all the neighbors of Germany are joining the Silk Road; it certainly greatly increases the pressure on those who are too stupid or too arrogant to see the potential this initiative has for German industry.

The Swiss Foreign Minister was just in China. He and his Chinese counterpart, Foreign Minister Wang Yi, and also State Councilor Yang Jiechi, declared that the collaboration of China and Switzerland in the New Silk Road is at the best historical level ever. They emphasized the importance of Xi Jinping's visit last year to Switzerland, when he addressed the Davos World Economic Forum as a keynote speaker, and then went on to Geneva, emphasizing the importance of Switzerland. So they're deepening the relationship between China and Switzerland.

Chinese President Xi Jinping holds a welcome ceremony for Zimbabwean President Emmerson Mnangagwa at the Great Hall of the People in Beijing, April 3, 2018.

And the Austrian government has a huge delegation, the largest ever: President Alexander Van der Bellen, Chancellor Sebastian Kurz, four cabinet ministers, and 170 CEOs from large corporations, are all spending five days in China. Kurz said that there is no ceiling when it comes to improving the relationship between Austria and China on the New Silk Road. The same thing is happening with Zimbabwe. The new President, Emmerson Mnangagwa, is going with a large delegation of 12 ministers and also many, many CEOs. Almost every day there is an interesting new breakout in relationships with China. As I have said many times, the Spirit of the New Silk Road is, in my view, absolutely unstoppable, unless we have World War III—which some people are risking.

Nevertheless, the idea of new relationships among nations, respecting each nation's sovereignty, respecting the difference in social systems, ending internationalist wars, and the idea of win-win cooperation—this is a new model of international relations and a New Paradigm. The biggest problem is that the Western media are so controlled by this insane geopolitical faction, that most people don't know enough about this new, growing model of win-win cooperation that is so rapidly involving more nations every day.

Join the Schiller Institute! Help us spread knowledge about the New Silk Road, and also the options to solve the present financial crisis, and many other crises around the world, with such an approach. I appeal to you: Don't sit on the fence! This is an incredibly important historic moment. The British have just suffered a terrible setback and defeat, which freaks them out. That British mistake and misjudgment is visible for everyone to see. We are in a very opportune moment to move forward and establish a completely different political, social, and economic system on this planet.

Schlanger: The Schiller Institute will be launching a new membership drive. If you want to increase the misery of the British intelligence establishment and the City of London, become a member of the Schiller Institute, and help us build the audience for these webcasts, to give an ever-increasing number of people an alternative to the lying media, which are otherwise the only option they have to allegedly find out about the world.

So Helga, I think that covers quite a bit. Thank you for joining us again, and we'll see you next week.

Zepp-LaRouche: Yes. Till next week.

hz.zepp@schiller-institut.de

The New Silk Road Becomes the World Land-Bridge

The BRICS countries have a strategy to prevent war and economic catastrophe. It's time for the rest of the world to join!

This 374-page report is a road-map to the New World Economic Order that Lyndon and Helga LaRouche have championed for over 20 years.

Includes:

Introduction by Helga Zepp-LaRouche, "The New Silk Road Leads to the Future of Mankind!"

The metrics of progress, with emphasis on the scientific principles required for survival of mankind: nuclear power and desalination; the fusion power economy; solving the water crisis.

The three keystone nations: China, the core nation of the New Silk Road; Russia's mission in North Central Eurasia and the Arctic; India prepares to take on its legacy of leadership.

Other regions: The potential contributions of Southwest, Central, and Southeast Asia, Australia, Europe, and Africa.

The report is available in PDF $35
and in hard copy $50 (softcover) $75 (hardcover)
plus shipping and handling.
Order from http://store.larouchepub.com

'The Campaign To Win the Future' Means Ending the Party Politics of the Past

by Susan Kokinda

EIR asked Susan Kokinda, a leading organizer for the Lyndon LaRouche Political Action Committee in the Midwest, to provide an account of the inspiration for, and response to LaRouche PAC's strategy for the 2018 elections. We thought it would be of interest to our readers. Here is Susan's response to our request.

April 8—In September 2012, during the run-up to a presidential election that featured a criminal Barack Obama and a hapless Mitt Romney, Lyndon LaRouche delivered a speech at his 90th birthday celebration in

EIRNS/Stuart Lewis

Lyndon LaRouche celebrating his 90th birthday.

which he called for the end of the party system that had coughed up those awful "choices." But, more than that, he presented the principles by which the nation should and could be governed, and by which American presidents should be selected.

LaRouche's speech presaged the political upheaval of 2016, which elected Donald Trump. The political upheaval of 2016 is a foreshadowing of the political and economic revolution which can free the nation from the British empire—this time permanently. "LaRouche PAC's 2018 Platform: The Campaign to Win the Future"

is the instrument to accomplish that. The "preamble" to the Platform reads as follows:

Our future could be determined by the 2018 Congressional elections. Neither party has a program to advance the nation, let alone ensure our short-term survival. **Therefore, we advance the following platform, and launch an independent expenditure campaign to make it happen.** We will campaign on the platform below, endorsing or opposing candidates, and creating large blocks of voters and candidates demanding this platform in critical Congressional Districts.

Presently, both major political parties are controlled by Wall Street. Both parties adhere to the post–World War II geopolitical system that has produced decades of perpetual war, and now threatens World War III by attacking China and Russia. The Democrats intend to use these elections to impeach the President. The Republicans, while nominally supporting the President, fanatically adhere to Wall Street's economic ideas which will destroy his Presidency....

The LaRouche platform has two flanks:

• End the coup against the President and prosecute those responsible.
• Implement LaRouche's Four Laws for Economic Recovery of the United States and join China's great Belt and Road Initiative for economic development. This will create millions of productive jobs, and ensure the United States joins a new paradigm of global collaboration on great infrastructure projects advancing the common aims of mankind.

Implicit in the 2018 Platform campaign is the realization of Lyndon LaRouche's 2012 explicit demand to eliminate the political parties. In fact, that campaign cannot be fully grasped without returning to, and examining LaRouche's earlier speech.

I remember the day the speech was delivered. A large group of LaRouche's closest associates were gathered on a Virginia hillside, overlooking valleys and the distant Blue Ridge Mountains. Greetings and congratulations from around the world, remembrances, and music had filled that late summer afternoon. Then LaRouche took the podium and sobered the gathering with a warning of the danger of thermonuclear war. He located that danger as coming from a dying British imperial system, and its control of the United States through its Wall Street spawn, its evil puppet Obama, and its hapless puppet Romney. The middle part of the speech soared, as he declared:

EIRNS/Eli Santiago

LaRouche PAC organizers in front of Senator Chuck Schumer's office in New York City.

> Human beings, as a species must be defended, because of the creativity that we represent, which means that we must defend that creativity, but we must also promote it. ... And it means that mankind has within its power, the power to do things which are beyond the imagination. We can explore the universe. We can explore, particularly, the Solar System. We know that we have the potential ability, innate in the nature of things, that mankind can begin to take over the Solar System.... These things are innate in the nature of mankind, the nature of mankind which many politicians have no sense of whatsoever. But we, as we live and die, as persons, must have the right to access to a meaningful course of life, to the ability to do something with our lives, which we can rest upon as we die, and know has something to do of permanent value for the human species. And *that* is what must be protected and defended.

Having had the privilege of listening to Lyndon LaRouche speak for over four decades, I expected the speech to stop on that beautiful note. But no, he was not done. At that point, he turned to "the politics of Earth, the politics of the United States," and went on to call for the elimination of the party system. "The party system was a travesty, which has corrupted, and, in part, destroyed the United States, by itself—by means of itself—over much of our nation's history. The idea of the party system is a form of degeneration which must be eliminated, if we are going to be able to cope with the real challenges, which mankind should be occupied with ... now."

The Trump election was a de facto rejection of the party system. Trump ran against the entire Republican establishment, and won election in key states with almost no help from the official Republican Party apparatus. The stunning lack of support for Trump as President from Republicans in Congress for his initiatives toward China and Russia and for federal funding for infrastructure, underscore the fact that, while he hijacked the Republican Party to get elected, he has no Republican support for the very policies which got him elected. Little need be said about the disintegration of the obstructionist Democratic Party, as evidenced by the mass migration of blue collar workers, especially in the Midwest, into the Trump camp.

Yet, as we head into the 2018 mid-term elections, the very people who caused this political realignment are lining up on the barricades of the party politics from which they broke from in 2016. As we talk to Trump supporters, who are mobilizing for local, state, and national Republican campaigns, and confront them with this reality, they immediately agree that the Republican Party is hostile to Trump, and the best they can hope for is that maybe they can elect a few candidates in the primaries who are loyal to him. Meanwhile many of the blue collar workers who voted for Trump are definitively *not* going to vote for a budget-cutting, single-issue-spouting Republican, and will instead turn to the Democratic primaries in hopes of finding a few sane Democrats, who will at least pay lip service to defending the working class.

If the American people stay in that box, then come November, they will end up with the choice of a bunch of Wall Street Democrats running against a bunch of Wall Street Republicans.

LaRouche addressed this in the 2012 speech: "But we don't want the top-down rule of a party system, which is controlled by the money sent to them, by financial interests which control money which gives one party advantage over the other! You want the bare citizen, as a citizen, to have an equal right, and independent of this party system."

That is the intention of LaRouche PAC's Platform fight: to organize the movement which rejected war and Wall Street in 2016, into an effective force demanding the economic and strategic policy which will fulfill the mandate of 2016, one completely divorced from party politics. In Michigan, LaRouche PAC organizers are bringing the Platform to every point of the political spectrum—to Democrat and Republican campaigns and political events, to Tea Party meetings, to trade unions, to the State Legislature. They are finding that the dividing line is not one of party; it is one of reality versus ideology. There are ideologues in both parties, who are living in the world of CNN or Fox TV or the *Wall Street Journal* or the *Huffington Post*.

There are those, however, who *do* respond with the recognition that, within the existing economic paradigm, *no one* has a solution to the underlying economic crisis, especially to the yawning infrastructure hole that the nation faces, let alone to a complete leap of the economy to a higher economic platform. When those responsive layers are presented with the dramatic transformation of China over the past 25 years, accomplished using the principles that are embodied in LaRouche's Four Laws, there is immediate resonance.

EIRNS/Bill Roberts

LaRouche Political Action Committee organizers.

This is what LaRouche called for in 2012:

And why should we be spending our time selecting a government of two parties, neither of which is fit to be our government. Why don't we have a national government selected in the way that George Washington, for example, President George Washington, had intended? We would not **have** that mess! And the citizen would be called upon, not to decide whose butt he wants to kiss, but rather what the issues and programs are that this citizen wishes to express. *We want to engage the citizen in the dialogue! We don't want to take the competition* ***between*** *groups of citizens.* We want the citizen to force the reality that he or she is voting for the government. And what the citizens do in voting for a government, will determine the fate of the nation.

We want to **confront** the citizen, with **his** or **her** responsibility for being accountable for what government is, and what it becomes. We have to **force** responsibility upon the individual citizen, as a citizen, not as a sucker, playing into some kind of game.

That is the purpose of the LaRouche PAC 2018 campaign: to confront the citizen with his or her responsibility for policy-making, and to provoke that process long before he or she walks into a voting booth. By doing so, the political realignment that emerged in the 2016 election will be coupled with the necessary revolution in economic policy.

Houston Mobilizes for Mankind's Shared Future

by Brian Lantz

April 7—Amidst the tensions and the potentials which now characterize events taking place on the world stage, the Schiller Institute held a dramatic public forum on April 4, in Houston, Texas, urging cooperation among nations to create "a new paradigm" for humanity. Held at the University of Houston, the daytime public forum was titled, "The New Silk Road—Peace through Economic Development," and subtitled "China's Worldwide 'Belt and Road Initiative'—The U.S. Can Join!" The event is surely producing wide ripple effects, given the present moment and the quality of participation in this forum.

Schiller Institute/Anastasia Mares

Left to right: Brian Lantz, Wang Yu, China Deputy Consul General in Houston, and Aisha Farooqui, Pakistan Deputy Consul General in Houston.

Following the April 2017 meeting between President Donald Trump and China's President Xi Jinping at Mar-a-Lago, Florida, and their second meeting during President Trump's November 2017 visit to Beijing, the potential for positive cooperation between the two nations is great.

The Schiller Institute is mobilizing support—nationally and internationally—for the critical next step, which must now take place to move the world in the right direction: President Trump must be empowered to place China's "New Silk Road" offer at the very center of both U.S. foreign and economic-recovery policy. Such action—clearing the way for major Chinese investment in the United States in the form of financing and opening up new markets for U.S. exports—will create the conditions for a rapid build-out of new U.S. infrastructure, and simultaneously spark a U.S. agro-industrial transformation. Houston—the nation's "energy capital," home to the second-largest U.S. port, and our fourth most populous city—is intimately entwined in the current global economic and political conflict.

Generations of Americans have been known for their "can-do" spirit, and it is still there, ready to be tapped: The University of Houston forum audience was *bowled over* by the April 4 presentations. "This is really big!" and "Why didn't I know about this?" came the excited responses. The day's panelists powerfully conveyed the great possibilities at our doorstep. The panelists were Ms. Aisha Farooqui, Consul General of the Islamic Republic of Pakistan in Houston; Mr. Wang Yu, PhD, Deputy Consul General of the People's Republic of China in Houston; and Brian Lantz, the event organizer, on behalf of the Schiller Institute.

Importantly, the sizable audience was a cross-section of a Houston which is transforming itself into an international city. Participants included hyphenated-Americans from around the globe—African-American, Hispanic, Pakistani, Chinese, Nigerian, Vietnamese, Hungarian, and other varieties of "Anglos." There were business men and business women, a number of students, attorneys, staff from the City of Houston's trade office, staff of a Texas State Representative, as well as long-time Schiller Institute activists, and the official participation of consular officials from five nations. Three participants had been part of Houston Mayor Turner's major trade mission to China last December. Press also attended, including a Houston monthly magazine focused on international affairs, and a Chinese news service.

Audience at the Houston Schiller Institute conference.

A Higher Calling

Kesha Rogers, speaking for the Schiller Institute, first set the stage with introductory remarks. Ms. Rogers began with a short video clip of Schiller Institute President Helga Zepp-LaRouche announcing the 2014 release of the *EIR* Special Report, *The New Silk Road Becomes the World Land-Bridge*, to promote the BRICS approach and President Xi Jinping's Belt and Road Initiative as the alternative to a war of extinction. Several people commented later that the video had immediately grabbed their full intention.

Kesha Rogers

April 4th was also the 50th anniversary of the assassination of Rev. Dr. Martin Luther King, Jr., and Rogers continued, quoting Dr. Martin Luther King on the "The World House": "All inhabitants of the globe are now neighbors," Dr. King had said, due to the revolutions in technology including in making war. King pressed on, Rogers recalled, showing that it was therefore in the interest of all people to put an end to all poverty and war.

Presenting the role of the Schiller Institute and Lyndon and Helga LaRouche in consciously carrying forward Rev. Martin Luther King, Jr.'s work, she held up the January, 1997 *EIR* Special Report, *The Eurasian Land-Bridge, The 'New Silk Road.'* The title itself clearly reflects the Institute's influence—over decades—in organizing a process that has taken wonderful form in China's President Xi Jinping's Belt and Road Initiative. The task is to end poverty by achieving peace through economic development, Rogers emphasized, and she urged everyone to join the Schiller Institute, and purchase the *EIR* and Schiller Institute's special reports.

The Silk Road in Action:
Whither the United States?

Ms. Rogers introduced Consul General Aisha Farooqui, a senior diplomat now representing the Islamic Republic of Pakistan from Houston. Texas is home to one of the largest Pakistani-American populations in the United States. Ms. Farooqui stated at the outset that she would "present the Belt and Road Initiative from Pakistan's perspective." She began by proudly presenting a brief picture of Pakistan as a nation-state rooted in ancient civilization and now a rapidly developing republic. As the world's sixth most populous country, with a population of which 60% are under 30 years of age, Pakistan has been achieving a 6% GDP growth rate over the last few years, and the industrial sector has been expanding at 6.8% percent with 1,000 active foreign companies. "Added to this is the significant advantage that we expect to accrue as a result of our strategic partnership with China."

Schiller Institute/Anastasia Mares
Aisha Farooqui
Consul General, Pakistan

Ms. Farooqui turned to the China-Pakistan Economic Development Corridor (CPEC) as a "flagship project" of China's Belt and Road, one that will shape a "21st Century model of economic development." She authoritatively presented the CPEC plan, using a number of maps and photos, so that the audience quickly grasped the size of the multiple projects involving highways, energy, rail, and ports, with $46 billion in investments. Students could be seen videoing the presentation on their phones, and clicks were heard from smart phones and cameras, capturing Consul General Farooqui's slides. Many in the audience were clearly hearing about all of this for the first time. Consul General Farooqui, a veteran diplomat with ambassadorial experience, made a big impact with her knowledge and gravitas.

China's Deputy Consul General in Houston, Dr. Wang Yu, followed. Dr. Wang, with a career in the Chinese Foreign Ministry and diplomatic postings, has been praised by Houston city officials for his role in overseeing the Mayor's December 2017 trade mission to China. Dr. Wang began by praising Consul General Farooqui's presentation. The Belt and Road Initiative (BRI) is, he emphasized, an *initiative*, not a project, and "not a regime." Mutual consultation, joint con-

Schiller Institute/Anastasia Mares
Dr. Wang Yu
Deputy Consul General, China

struction, and shared benefit lie at the heart of the BRI, and it thereby represents a new path for global development. It is both open-ended and open to everyone, including the United States, which China hopes will join.

China is pursuing a policy "of harmony and inclusiveness—we are not imposing anything—and one which is market-oriented, based on mutual benefit and local employment," Dr. Wang explained. This can be seen in China's commitment to "integration" of its Belt and Road with other national and regional strategies. He pointed to China's integration with the Eurasian Economic Union led by Russia, and also with South Korea. "South Korea has its own strategy, and we're making our own adaptations," Wang said. "We are resolute; we are determined to integrate China's economy with regionalization."

In his dignified, low-key presentation, Dr. Wang focused on making China's intentions crystal clear and thereby defusing any misunderstandings. He also stressed the cultural and social dimensions of creating "a better environment." His effectiveness was highlighted when he projected a slide that read, "U.S.-China Cooperation," with the national flags of the United States and China highlighted against a dramatic background. All the cameras and smart phones in the room seemed to go off again at once! Clearly this was what the audience wanted to know more about.

Brian Lantz, on behalf of the Schiller Institute, was the last speaker, and outlined the enormous potentials of America-China "Silk Road" cooperation. First, Lantz provoked the audience to grasp that the world was, at that moment, being fundamentally changed, as witness the presentations by Consul General Fa-

Schiller Institute/Anastasia Mares
Brian Lantz

rooqui and Dr. Wang. *Trillions of dollars equivalent* in investment are now being invested around the world through the Belt and Road, Lantz underscored. A slide of a now-iconic photo of Houston's overwhelmed reservoirs during Hurricane Harvey went up on the screen, followed by slides showing the topology of the Gulf Coast region. Clearly, "hundreds of billions of dollars of investment" are required to permanently address this situation—not a patch here and a patch there.

Comparing that requirement to China's projects at home, and in Africa and the Americas, allowed the audience to see for themselves the disparity, and what could be done with the BRI approach. But where would the money come from? Lantz compared what China's state owned enterprises (SOEs) had done with roughly $15 trillion invested since 2008, and what the U.S. government, banks, and corporations had done with a similar amount. China Railway, for example, now owns 24,000 km of high-speed rail. American corporations, on the other hand, through "financial engineering," . . . have doubled their corporate debt!

We clearly have to change our thinking, Lantz emphasized: "China is ready to invest, if we clear the way by creating the needed national credit institutions. Then we can rebuild!" Recall that moment when John F. Kennedy spoke at Rice University, and set the goal of going to the moon "within this decade." Recall that we actually did it. We have to think that way, and act that way, again.

Through the 'Lens' of a New Paradigm

As the reader can imagine, questions and discussion quickly ensued, and continued until the last minute the room was available. The first question, from a businessman, was on China's willingness to build its high-speed rail in Texas and make similar investments. Another, related question was on the role of "private investments" and how private enterprise can get involved in the New Silk Road.

Dr. Wang, the Deputy Consul General, responded by gracefully stating that China had offered its knowledge and experience, and was open to further participation—but "both sides" had to be willing, and that it was now up to the American side. Dr. Wang also wryly commented on the problem of the U.S. "federal security check" that is blocking fuller Chinese company investments and U.S.-China company collaboration in U.S. projects. He also pointed to the upcoming Houston Innovation Summit, to which tech startups are invited to make their pitch to three hundred Chinese companies

looking to invest. He also advertised the upcoming November 5-10, 2018 International Import Expo in Shanghai, organized by the Ministry of Commerce. U.S. companies are invited to come and promote their products for potential export to China. Thousands of companies are expected.

As the event concluded, many audience members rushed to the front of the room, expressing their happiness and excitement to continue the discussion with the speakers and each other. Discussion continued throughout the room. "How do we get involved in this; why aren't we involved in this?" exclaimed a young Chinese businessman, originally met at a Lunar New Year festival. An experienced aide to a state legislator, who could be seen taking detailed notes throughout, was personally flummoxed. "I am really glad you invited me! Why don't people know about this!? We've been fighting these wars and keeping Wall Street happy, but. . . ." He wants future discussion with the legislator and himself, on the New Silk Road potential and really solving Houston's infrastructure crisis.

A business woman walked up to the Schiller Institute literature table. "I want those two reports!" she exclaimed. A 29-year-old with a master's degree in sociology, who has written on the migrant crisis, "clicked" on the connection between the regime-change wars and the global refugee crisis, with the New Paradigm of the "Silk Road" as the solution. A Houston city official approached the speakers to praise the event as a contribution to fulfilling the potential of the Mayor's recent trade mission to China. A formerly standoffish diplomat came forward with his "thumbs up." He now wants to arrange a Schiller Institute meeting with his new Consul General. Press were doing interviews and taking more photographs. Everyone was very, very happy.

The consular representatives all made their pleasure known. One commented on how much he had learned; a Chinese consul commented on "how successful and well organized" the event was; an experienced diplomat volunteered that he had been struck, over time, by the Schiller Institute's commitment to "a process," i.e., maintaining its principled focus. One of the speakers commented that no one would believe that the introduction and three presentations had not been closely coordinated for overall effect—when actually each had been prepared quite separately under hectic schedules.

The Silk Road Reaches Africa

We present here an edited version of Chapter Two, "The Silk Road Reaches Africa," from the 246 page Special Report Extending the New Silk Road to West Asia and Africa—A vision of an Economic Renaissance, *published by the Schiller Institute in November 2017. The full Special Report is available for purchase at* http://newparadigm.schillerinstitute.com/extending-new-silk-road-west-asia-africa/

In May 2014, while on a tour to several African nations, Chinese Premier Li Keqiang projected an optimistic vision of Chinese-aided industrial and infrastructural growth for the African continent. His tour started in Ethiopia, ended in Kenya, and included Angola, China's biggest African trading partner, and Nigeria, its third-biggest. Contrary to frustrated and nervous reporting in Western media and think tanks, Li was not on a shopping spree for raw materials.[1] Rather, he advocated an increase in Chinese industrial investment in Africa, and Chinese-aided infrastructure construction, policies that will raise standards of living, and propel Africa into a new economic platform.

Speaking at the African Union headquarters in Addis Ababa, Ethiopia, on May 5, Li emphasized that one of China's goals is to fulfill the dream of connecting

China News

Chinese Premier Li Keqiang speaking at a joint press conference with East African leaders in Nairobi on May 11, 2014.

all African capitals with high-speed rail, to boost pan-African communication and development. Li emphasized that China has developed world-class technologies in this field.

This is the first time that a leading nation has advocated a plan for extensive industrial and infrastructural development of Africa, since Lyndon LaRouche initiated a study in 1979 calling for the rapid development of infrastructure, including a continent-wide rail network, ambitious water projects, nuclear power, and industrialization.

China has taken the lead in building transport and power infrastructure throughout Africa. One of the most significant outcomes during Li's tour was the signing by the China Railway Construction Corp of a $13.1 billion deal with the Nigerian Ministry of Transport to build a coastal railway in Nigeria, from Lagos to Calabar, reported by the May 10 *People's Daily Online* to be one of the largest foreign railway projects China has ever signed.[2] The report cited the head of the Rail-

---

1. See, for example, the commentary by Dr. Alex Vines, published by the British Chatham House, "Premier Li Keqiang in Africa: The Importance of Angola for China." (https://www.chathamhouse.org/expert/comment/14134) Another, more hostile article in the *New York Review of Books* titled, "The Chinese Invade Africa," stated: "Groups such as Human Rights Watch have detailed labor abuses and shown how China's limits on free speech at home have been exported abroad, especially to dependent states in regions like Africa. The economic ties are sometimes portrayed as under-the-table deals cut between Beijing and corrupt leaders in Africa. Instead of helping to build civil society, these deals are said to hurt Africa's long-term interests, reinforcing the tendency of corrupt elites to secure resources at a low price." (http://www.nybooks.com/articles/2014/09/25/chinese-invade-africa/)

---

2. Lu Yanan, "China and Nigeria sign a $13.1 billion rail deal," http://en.people.cn/business/8623229.html

Launch of the standard gauge Mombasa to Nairobi railway, in Mombasa, May 2017.

way Bureau of Nigeria, who said that the company will build a 1,385 km single-track line for trains that will run at up to 120 km per hour. The Lagos-Kano Standard Gauge Railway was officially opened in July 2016, and work on the Lagos-Ibadan section began in March 2017.

Another major development was the agreement reached in Kenya on May 11, 2014 between the Chinese delegation and the leaders of the East African Community (EAC), to build a $3.8 billion rail link between Kenya's Indian Ocean port city of Mombasa and the capital, Nairobi, as the first stage of a line that will eventually link Uganda, Rwanda, Burundi, South Sudan and Ethiopia. Under the terms of the agreement, the Exim Bank of China provided 90% of the cost to replace the crumbling British colonial-era line, the "Lunatic Express," with a 609.3 km modern standard-gauge railway. The remaining 10% is Kenya's responsibility. Construction began in late October 2014 with China Communications Construction Company as the lead contractor, and the line was completed nearly a year ahead of schedule, in May 2017.

The new Mombasa-Nairobi (Kenya) line has cut passenger travel time from twelve hours to around four.

The signing ceremony for this rail line agreement was attended by Premier Li, Kenya's President Uhuru Kenyatta, Uganda's President Yoweri Museveni, Rwanda's President Paul Kagame, South Sudan's President Salva Kiir, and high-level representatives of Burundi and Tanzania. "This project demonstrates that there is equal cooperation and mutual benefit between China and the East African countries, and the railway is a very important part of transport infrastructure development," Premier Li said. Kenyatta hailed the booming relationship with China, calling it one "based on mutual trust," and saying Kenya "has found an honorable partner in China." President Museveni took a shot at Western powers saying, "We are happy to see that China is concentrating on the real issues of development. They don't give lectures on how to run local governments."

This agreement is just one of a series—there are similar agreements with Nigeria, Angola, and Tanzania, for railways, ports, power generation, and industrial projects—that China has signed to connect Africa to the BRI and build development corridors that can propel the economies of Africa into the 21st Century.

Another landmark achievement in Africa was the completion of the Addis Ababa-Djibouti 750 km electrified Standard Gauge Railway in October 2016. It connects land-locked Ethiopia and its 90 million population to world transport routes and the Maritime Silk Road through the Port of Djibouti. Construction was started after an agreement was signed in 2011 between the Ethiopian Railway Corporation and the Chinese construction corporations CREC and CRCC. The project was financed with a $3 billion loan extended by the Exim Bank of China. This railway is part of a very ambitious Ethiopian plan for industrialization, the Growth and Transformation Plan, which includes a national railway network connecting the major cities of the country, the development of five major industrial zones, and water, power and agricultural projects.

China in Africa: Myths or Facts

A June 2017 report by the global consultancy McKinsey & Company revealed stunning facts about China's level of economic engagement with Africa, and refuted many myths about that involvement. The report,

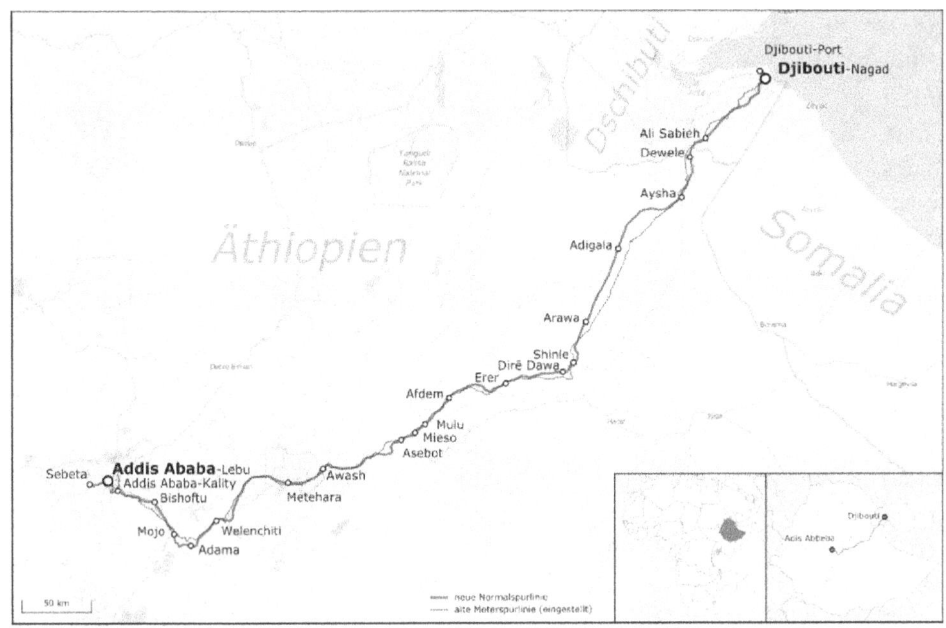

The Addis Ababa-Djibouti rail line.

titled *Dance of the Lions and Dragons*,[3] is based on surveys of 1,000 Chinese firms in eight African countries.

The study reported the following:

• China's involvement in Africa far exceeds estimates provided by Chinese official statistics.

• In the past two decades, China has become Africa's largest economic partner, with annual goods trade in 2015 reaching $180 billion, compared to the other large partners of Africa: India (59 billion), France (57 billion), the United States (53 billion), and Germany (46 billion). Trade has been growing at approximately 20 percent per year.

• Chinese foreign direct investment has grown even faster over the past decade, with an annual growth rate of 40 percent.

• China is also a large and fast-growing source of aid.

• China is the largest source of "construction financing for many of Africa's most ambitious infrastructure developments in recent years."

• Ten thousand Chinese firms are active in Africa. Around 90 percent of these firms are privately owned, contrary to the reports that giant state-owned firms are dominant.

• A third of these firms are involved in manufacturing, handling an "estimated 12 percent of Africa's industrial production—valued at some $500 billion a year in total."

• Contrary to allegations of Chinese grabbing of African natural resources, the study shows that the activity of these firms is not focused on exporting goods out of Africa, but rather producing to meet the growing demand in Africa itself.

• In infrastructure, Chinese firms handle 50 percent of Africa's internationally contracted construction market.

• The common perception of Chinese firms bringing hundreds of thousands of Chinese laborers to Africa, rather than employing locals, is refuted. Among the 1,000 Chinese companies surveyed, 89% of the employees were African, adding up to nearly 300,000 jobs for African workers. Projecting these figures to all 10,000 Chinese firms in Africa, this suggests that Chinese-owned businesses employ several million Africans!

• Furthermore, 44% of the managers at these firms are Africans.

• Some form of skills training is provided by 64% of the Chinese employers. In companies engaged in construction and manufacturing, where skilled labor is a necessity, half offer apprenticeship training.

• Chinese companies are actively transferring technology to Africa, and in many cases are lowering the prices of sophisticated technology and machinery by as much as 40%, making them affordable in Africa.

Unfortunately, and in a way that reveals the currently dominant mindset of Western financial institutions, the same McKinsey & Company report itself, after having detailed all the fascinating things China has accomplished through state-backed public credit, recommends that this form of financing should be abandoned, and instead African nations and China should "Switch to PPP" (public private partnership) financing.[4]

---

3. McKinsey & Company, *Dance of the Lions and Dragons: How are Africa and China engaging, and how will the partnership evolve?*, June 2017 (http://www.mckinsey.com/global-themes/middle-east-and-africa/the-closest-look-yet-at-chinese-economic-engagement-in-africa)

4. Ibid., page 69, Exhibit 21, key recommendation number 10. We discuss the problematic PPP model of financing infrastructure in Chapter 4.

Who Is Out To Control Africa's Mining Sector?

Contrary to what is generally believed, China is not the largest foreign investor in Africa. China ranks third, after the United States and the United Kingdom. In the ten years between 2005 and 2014, the total accumulated Chinese direct investment (FDI) in Africa was below $40 billion, while that of the U.S. was above $60 billion, and that of the U.K. over $50 billion. However, China is both the number one trade partner of Africa and leads in the rate of growth of direct investments in the recent years; this means it will soon surpass the United States and the UK. On the other hand, U.S. investments in Africa have been collapsing at a rapid rate starting in 2009, when President Barack Obama was elected.

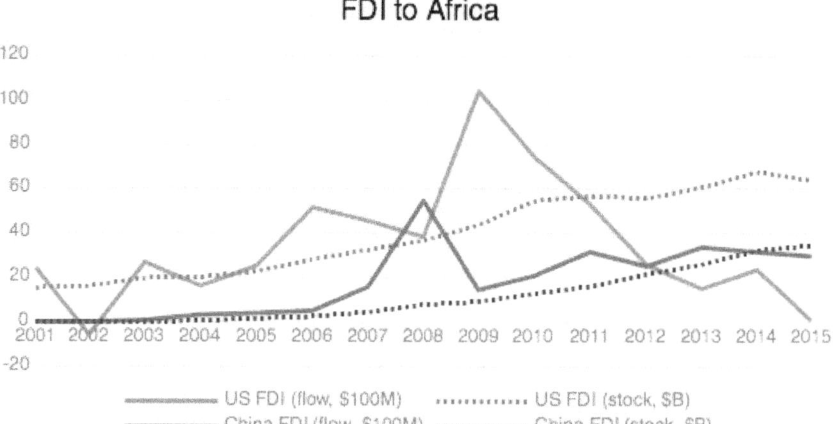

Source: SAIS-CARI analysis, based on data from: UNCTAD Bilateral FDI Statistics; China Statistical Yearbook; Statistical Bulletin of China's Outward Foreign Direct Investment; Bureau of Economic Analysis, US Department of Commerce.

The statistics reveal that it is not China but rather the United States and the UK which are primarily interested in the raw materials and financial wealth of Africa.

While China's investments are spread over several economic sectors in Africa, with infrastructure construction being the primary one, U.S. and British investments are concentrated in raw materials and finance.

The Chinese Exim Bank is increasingly becoming the leading source of foreign loans to infrastructure and other projects in Africa, with more than $50 billion over the period from 2005 to 2014; during the same time, the U.S. Exim Bank had invested less than one-tenth of that amount in Africa, and 70% of those investments were directed to the mining sector.

A report issued by the China Africa Research Initiative, at the Johns Hopkins School of Advanced International Studies—along with other studies—provides a useful quantitative overview of U.S. and Chinese investments into Africa.

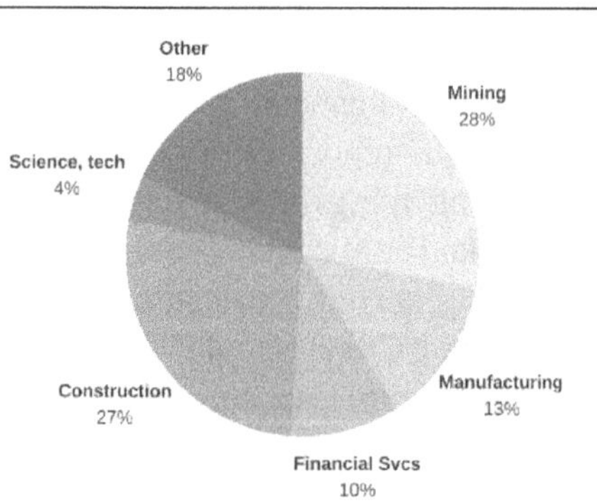

Source: SAIS-CARI analysis, based on data from: UNCTAD Bilateral FDI Statistics; China Statistical Yearbook; Statistical Bulletin of China's Outward Foreign Direct Investment; Bureau of Economic Analysis, US Department of Commerce.

US FDI Stock to Africa by Sector, 2015

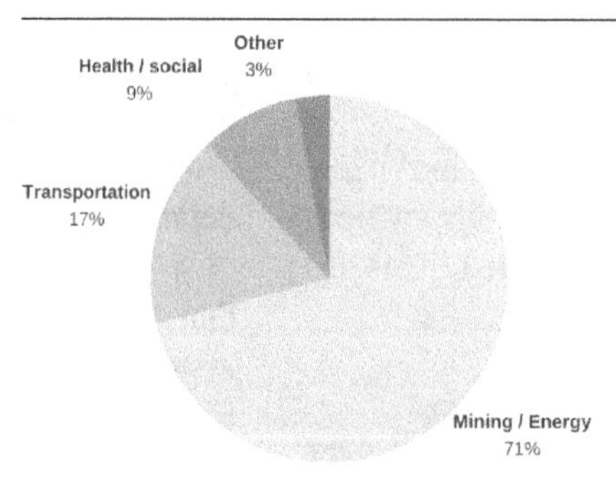

US Exim Bank Loans to Africa by Sector, 2005-2015

Source: SAIS-CARI, policy brief #18, based on data from CARI's Loan Database and the US Eximbank.

The Eurasia Canal

by Dean Andromidas

April 9—National economies that have no direct access to the sea, or access via river and canal waterways, are always at a serious disadvantage. A glance at the most productive region in Europe, the Paris-Berlin-Vienna "Productive Triangle," shows it to be integrated with a dense network of super-highways and railroads, but also with interconnecting river and canal networks that provide efficient and inexpensive transportation of bulk cargoes, including mineral ores, chemicals, and hydrocarbon products, as well as the less time-sensitive among containerized cargoes.

A glance at the map of Eurasia reveals that its vast, landlocked central region is its least developed. The geographical situation is similar to that of the North American continent, where the Great Lakes reach almost to the midpoint of the continent. These vast "inland seas" were first connected to the world's oceans by the Erie Canal. There followed the linking-up of all five Great Lakes with a system of canals and locks. Ultimately, the Saint Lawrence Seaway permitted 28,000-ton, ocean-going ships to reach the Lake Superior

St. Lawrence Seaway.

DOT

Projected route of the Eurasia Canal.

port of Duluth, Minnesota, almost midway across the continent. This was a process of development that took more than 150 years to complete, but that process helped to industrialize both the United States and Canada.

The Mediterranean, the Black, and the Caspian seas similarly stretch halfway across Eurasia, bringing together three continents—Asia, Africa, and Europe. While the Mediterranean and the Black seas are connected through the Dardanelles and the Bosporus, the Caspian is connected to them only through the very low-capacity and inconvenient Volga-Don Canal in the Russian Federation. The remedy is to cut a ship canal across the Russian Caucasus through the Russian Federation's republics of Kalmykia and Dagestan, the oblasts of Astrakhan and Volgograd, and the Rostov and Stavropol regions, along the Kuma-Manych Depression, thereby linking the Caspian with the Sea of Azov and on to the Black Sea. It was a mere 18,000 years ago that this depression served as a strait, the Manych Strait, connecting the two seas.

The Russian Czar's en-

Lock No. 14, Volga-Don Canal.

cc/Dmitry Nikolenko

gineers dreamt of building such a canal, and the engineers of the Soviet Union, under orders from Stalin, began construction of the Kuma-Manych Canal in 1932. Work stopped because of the outbreak of World War II. After the war, the project was downgraded to an irrigation canal, and then completely halted in 1989 by environmentalists in the government of Mikhail Gorbachov. While much of canal still exists, it is in very poor condition.

During his annual national address in April 2007, Russian President Vladimir Putin called for modernizing the Volga-Don and Volga-Baltic canals. He proposed that the government "examine the establishment of an international consortium to build a second section of the Volga-Don Canal." This new transport artery would have a significant impact, improving shipping links between the Caspian and the Black seas.

"Not only would this give the Caspian Sea countries a route to the Black Sea and the Mediterranean, thus providing them with access to the world's oceans," said Putin, "it would also radically change their geopolitical situation by enabling them to become sea powers." This proposal is called the Volga-Don 2 Canal.

Speaking at a conference of foreign investors on June 15, 2007, the President of Kazakhstan, Nursultan Nazarbayev, proposed the construction of a Eurasia Canal through the Manych Depression, declaring, "We need different routes: naturally, these commodities—oil and gas—will follow the routes that will prove to be economically sound for us. The construction of a new 'Eurasia' shipway from the Caspian to the Black Sea can become a landmark project.... This canal would be a powerful outlet for the entire Central Asia seaward across Russia."[1]

The two presidents soon met on the subject, resulting in the commissioning of a feasibility study comparing the two projects, which was carried out with financing provided by the Eurasian Development Bank. The study concluded that a ship canal through the Manych Depression was economically feasible, and would also benefit the development of the Russian Caucasus by providing employment and improving the region's agricultural potential.

In 2009, President Nazarbayev recruited the support of China for the project, and in August 2009, during an

---

1. See https://jamestown.org/program/the-kazakh-russian-eurasia-canal-the-geopolitics-of-water-transport-and-trade/

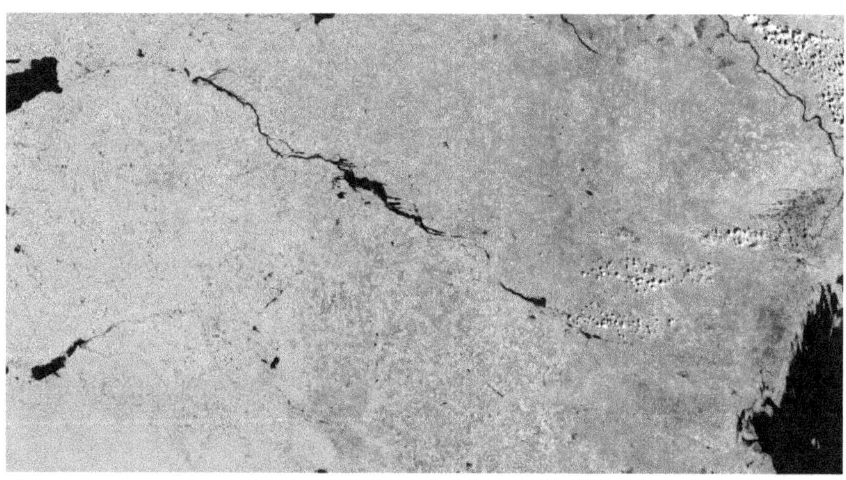

cc

Satellite photo of the Kuma-Manych Depression and Manych River.

The Kazakh-Russian "Eurasia" Canal: The Geopolitics of Water, Transport, and Trade

Publication: Eurasia Daily Monitor Volume: 7 Issue: 177
By: Roman Muzalevsky

October 1, 2010 07:25 PM Age: 8 years

The Proposed Eurasian Canal.

The Kazakh-Russian joint working group will soon present a proposal for the construction of the "Eurasia" canal linking the Caspian and Azov seas (www.izvestia.ru, September 28). From expanded trade and transit across Eurasia to new energy projects and maritime access for landlocked Central Asia, the project entails far-reaching geopolitical ramifications, with Russia, Kazakhstan, and China, among others, standing to benefit from growing energy trade and economic relations between Europe and Asia. With an estimated price tag of 4.5 billion Euros and annual freight transit capacity of 75 million tons, the 700 kilometer long planned waterway, according to one version, traverses Russia's areas of Dagestan, Kalmykia, Stavropol, and Rostov

official visit to China, the President of the Russian Republic of Kalmykia, Kirsan Ilyumzhinov, a political ally of President Putin, signed a letter of intent with Sinohydro, a Chinese hydropower, engineering, and construction company, to secure its participation in building the Eurasia Canal, which also resulted in a preliminary feasibility study.[2]

The 2008 financial crisis and the failure of the Russian government to come to a decision, led both the Volga-Don 2 project and the Eurasia Canal to be frozen, despite the keen interest of Kazakhstan.

In the meantime, in 2001, the European Union, as part of an effort to isolate Russia, had organized the Transport Corridor Europe Caucasus Asia (TRACECA) Intergovernmental Commission (IGC) of all the former Soviet Central Asian Republics and others, including Azerbaijan, Armenia, Georgia, Kazakhstan, Kyrgyzstan, Moldova, Tajikistan, Ukraine, and Uzbekistan, as well as Bulgaria, Romania, and Turkey. China and Russia were not included.

The absence of Russia signaled that the EU and the West did not support the Eurasia Canal. Instead, they worked on developing a road and rail corridor through mountainous Azerbaijan and Georgia. Since rail and roadways already existed, this approach entailed minimal investment, while failing to solve the basic problem that would be addressed by a new waterway.

The Belt and Road Initiative Can Make the Difference

In 2013, Chinese President Xi Jinping launched what is now known as the Belt and Road Initiative (BRI), thereby opening new potential for the realization of a Eurasian canal project. In the Russian Federation, the former President of Kalmykia, Kirsan Ilyumzhinov, had embraced the BRI, and on November 11, 2016, he presented the project for a transport corridor called "Eurasia" at the Eurasian Economic Integration conference in Moscow, where the Eurasia Canal was featured. Moreover, the continuing strengthening of ties between Putin and Xi could induce Russia to take more action on the project.[3]

In 2017, a significant short study, "The Eurasia Canal as a Factor of Economic Prosperity for the Caspian Region," appeared in the Kazakh journal, *Geography, Environment, Sustainability*, written by Nuraly Bekturganov of Kazakhstan's Academy of Natural Sciences and Arasha V. Bolaev, adviser to the President of the Russian Academy of Sciences.

The two authors correctly assert that China's Belt and Road Initiative and its commitment to rapidly develop its western regions have dramatically shifted the

---

2. See   https://www.fide.com/component/content/article/1-fide-news/4098--working-visit-of-fide-president-kirsan-ilyumzhinov-to-beijing.html

3. See   http://kirsan.today/en/analytics/item/1175-ilyumzhinov-s-project-the-new-silk-road.html

situation. They add, "The Eurasia Canal construction project is consistent with the spirit of the One Belt One Road initiative, as the route 'western China-Kazakhstan-Caspian Sea-Eurasia Canal-the Black Sea' will be the shortest between China and the European Union."

The region of Central Asia that constitutes the "market" for a canal easily encompasses more than a billion people. The riparian countries alone include Kazakhstan, with 18 million; Uzbekistan, whose western border is a mere 200 km from the Caspian, with 32 million; Turkmenistan with 5.7 million; Iran with 80 million; Azerbaijan with 10 million; and of course Russia, in which a sizable part of its 165 million citizens live in this area. There is also Afghanistan with 35 million; Tajikistan with 9 million; and Kyrgyzstan with 6 million, which will also benefit from the canal.

The canal could also be part of a new trade route for Urumqi, the capital of China's westernmost Xinjiang region (population 24 million), which is almost equally distant from the eastern shore of the Caspian Sea and China's eastern sea coast.

In effect, all cargo traffic destined to and from the Mediterranean, thus including Europe, Africa and even the east coast of the Americas, will benefit.

According to Bekturganov and Bolaev, freight transportation capacity will need to increase to 75 million tons per year over the next decade. The capacity of the Don-Volga Canal is currently less than 15 million tons, the vast majority of which is taken up by Russian cargoes. Ships larger than 5,000 tons cannot pass through it.

With estimated oil reserves of 24 to 26 billion tons, this region accounts for 6 to 10% of world reserves. It has an estimated 8.3 trillion cubic meters of gas reserves. The transport of hydrocarbons via such a canal would add to its existing exports of 25 to 50 million tons per year. While pipelines can transport oil and gas, refined products are best transported by ship.

Cargo from the region not associated with hydrocarbons is estimated at 20 to 25 million tons, the vast majority being currently transported by road and rail. Much of the region's exports are bulk cargoes, including 4.5 million tons of grain exports from Kazakhstan alone. This region is also rich in mineral resources, which are expensive to extract and transport, due to lack of water transport.

A Eurasia Canal will clearly lead to a dramatic increase in cargoes from China and other countries that would normally ship via China's east coast ports or by rail. A research study by Sinohydro found that by 2030, 24 to 30 million tons of Chinese cargoes that would otherwise be transported through Chinese ocean ports, would be diverted to the canal, and 43 to 51 million tons by 2050.

In terms of viability, compare the highly successful Rhine-Main-Danube canal, which carries 6 million tons per year, and the Saint Lawrence Seaway, which carries 40 to 50 million tons.

Revolutionizing Navigation on the Caspian

The revolutionary potential of the Belt and Road Initiative in Central Asia demands a solution that will also revolutionize maritime transport. The largest ships now plying the waters of the Caspian, for example, the so called "river-sea" class vessels, are no larger than 10,000 to 13,000 deadweight tons, primarily because they are the largest ships able to navigate the Russian inland waterway network. By contrast, ships up to

100,000 tons, the largest size that can traverse the Bosporus Strait and Dardanelles, operate in the Black Sea.

The initial canal proposals called for a canal with the limited parameters of the river-sea ships of the 10,000 to 13,000 ton class.

The author of the Sinohydro report and the Bekturganov-Bolaev team concur that a canal should be modeled after that of the Great Lakes and Saint Lawrence Seaway, which can accommodate ships as large as 20,000 to 26,000 tons, the so-called Seawaymax or Handysize class. This class of ship is far more cost-effective for carrying cargoes to transshipment ports on the Black Sea, especially to the Port of Constanta, Romania at the entrance of the Danube-Black Sea Canal, where cargoes can be transferred to barges and enter the European inland waterway network. They could also sail directly to the ports of the Mediterranean and beyond the Pillars of Hercules, to destinations anywhere on the Seven Seas.

wikipedia

Handysize bulk carrier vessel COPAN in Bosporus waters.

The Eurasia Canal will require a two-way channel and locks to accommodate ships up to 226 m long, with a width of 24 m and a draft of 7.15 m. At a required length of 750 km, it will not be much longer than the 600 km Saint Lawrence Seaway, including the canals and locks connecting the five Great Lakes.

The topography of the Kuma-Manych Depression is almost ideal for canal construction, and will require far fewer locks than the Great Lakes and Saint Lawrence Seaway (15) and the 172 km Rhine-Main-Danube Canal (16).

The Caspian Sea is 27 m lower than the Black and Azov seas. The watershed between the Sea of Azov and the Caspian Sea has an elevation of 27 m on its western slope and 54 m on the east slope. This compares to the watershed between the Main and Danube rivers, which require lifting and lowering ships 176 m. The Eurasia Canal will require three shipping locks of low pressure on the western slope, and three of average pressure or six of low pressure on the eastern slope.

Until now, it has been proposed to use the remains of the old Manych Ship-Irrigation Canal, which includes the Manych River and a series of artificial lakes and reservoirs which would have to be connected and deepened.

There are also challenges to be overcome for water for the canal, requiring the erection of dams and the possibility of transferring water from the Volga River.

Bekturganov and Bolaev suggest building an entirely new construction parallel to the old structures. A cement-lined canal will enable better management of water resources that could be integrated in a regional system of optimal management, to improve the ecosystem and benefit the industry, agriculture and fisheries sectors.

The cost of the Eurasia Canal has been estimated to be between $4.5 and 17 billion, depending on the design parameters. This cost must be measured against the tremendous benefits accruing not only to the people of the vast region of Central Asia and China, but to those well beyond, as a new development corridor stretching from the Mediterranean and through the Black and Caspian seas is created.

Initially proposed in the 1890s, it wasn't until 1954 that the United States and Canada broke ground to jointly develop the Saint Lawrence Seaway. The 50-year delay was primarily due to opposition from vested interests, including railway companies and ocean port operators—not costs. It took very strong leadership by President Dwight D. Eisenhower to finally break through this blockage and get the project off the drawing-boards.

Similarly, vested interests are attempting to block the Eurasia Canal, the most serious of which are the European Union and other "Western" interests fixated on a policy of isolating Russia, and which see the BRI as a threat to their old imperial interests. Once this geopolitical opposition is overcome—and it will be overcome—a new path will be opened to integrate Eurasia.

A DIALOGUE OF THREE PRESIDENCIES

Bending the Arc of the Moral Universe Toward Justice

by Helga Zepp-LaRouche

This is the edited transcript of Helga Zepp-LaRouche's keynote address to the Schiller Institute conference in New York City, April 7, 2018. The conference took its name from the title of this address. The video is available.

Hello to all of you. I'm very happy to talk to you, at least via video, so I can share my ideas with you.

The Skripal Affair

In recent weeks, many people, in many countries, have been very distraught about the so-called Skripal affair. This was the assassination attempt, the poison gas attack on the former double agent Sergei Skripal and his daughter. The Theresa May government immediately accused Russia of carrying out the attack. I think that this particular situation has demonstrated, in a way we have never seen before, the role of the British empire, the British government, and British policies in the present escalation against Russia, and in a certain sense against China.

This affair was immediately made a NATO issue, and an issue for the European Union. Many EU members immediately declared unconditional solidarity with Theresa May. They agreed on the formulation that there is no other plausible explanation than that Russia did it. I think this reaction is very telling, because it shows the degree of British control in NATO, and in part of the European Union. Fortunately, about half of the European Union members did not agree. It also demonstrated the incredible, Orwellian character of the present Western democracies of the so-called "liberal"

EIRNS/Christopher Lewis

Helga Zepp-LaRouche addressing the April 7, 2018 Schiller Institute conference via video, in New York City.

Western system. Because the fact that these nations immediately abandoned the principle of *in dubio pro reo*, of innocence until proven guilty, and that truth was replaced by a consensus among countries, is quite telling. If that is the principle of international policy, then we are all in very bad shape.

The immediate danger is that this will not just lead to mass expulsions of diplomats. The United States expelled 60 diplomats, the British expelled a similar number, and Germany four. There were about 23 diplomats expelled from the other European countries. The danger is that this could lead to a broader escalation of confrontation with Russia and possibly even war. This is prewar propaganda.

Labour Says It Seems Boris Johnson "Misled" The Public Over The Skripal Nerve Agent

The foreign secretary is under fire from Labour and his Russian counterpart after both he and a now-deleted Foreign Office tweet said that scientists had confirmed the nerve agent used to poison Sergei Skripal and his daughter originated in Russia.

Originally posted on April 3, 2018, at 12:45 p.m.
Updated on April 4, 2018, at 11:39 a.m.

Patrick Smith
BuzzFeed News Reporter

UK Foreign Secretary Boris Johnson.

First of all, it is noteworthy that the two Skripals fortunately seem to be in much better condition. That raises a whole bunch of questions because if it was Novichok nerve gas, then the question is: How did the British so quickly provide an antidote such that the two victims are now happily surviving? Or, maybe it was not Novichok. How could they so quickly come to the conclusion that it was Russia, when Scotland Yard said it would take several weeks to find out what really was the nerve gas agent used in this attack?

As for the timing, the Skripal affair took place at precisely the point at which—in the United States—the whole focus of congressional investigations by the House Intelligence Committee, the House Judiciary Committee, similar committees in the Senate, was on the role of the British empire in the Russiagate affair, or the Trumpgate, or the Muellergate, depending on what you want to call it. This focus, by several committees, started to really put into the limelight the role of Christopher Steele, the so-called "former" MI6 agent, and therefore the role of the British government, and the collusion of Mueller with the British, in the attempt to organize a coup against President Trump.

So the timing of the Skripal affair was very convenient, because all of a sudden, the Russia issue was again dominant. Before the Skripal affair, you could say that the days of Theresa May seemed to be numbered, because she was in such an unstable position.

Cui Bono?

Now, *cui bono*? Who has the motive? In whose interest would such an affair be? Well, Russia really has no motive; why would this occur just weeks before the presidential election in Russia? Would Putin really want to have such notoriety just before the election, and just before the Soccer World Cup? In addition, Russia also would have had many opportunities to kill Skripal; he spent many years in a Russian jail. He also lived for many years in Great Britain without any problem. Nevertheless, despite that, Merkel and Macron, and half of the EU immediately came out saying, "No, the only plausible explanation is that it was Russia."

Boris Johnson, the Foreign Secretary, gave an interview to a German radio broadcaster, *Deutsche Welle*, in which he said that he had absolute, scientific proof from the scientists of the Porton Down laboratory, who had said that they definitely had 100% proof that it was Russia. In the meantime, the scientists refused to provide the after-the-fact evidence, and the head of the lab, Mr. Gary Aitkenhead, said that they could identify that it was Novichok, but that they could not identify the source or the origin of this poison gas. This was a very lamentable situation, so the Foreign Office immediately deleted the tweet in which this was stated, which leaves Boris Johnson standing there as a liar. That does not prevent the Theresa May government from continuing to push the lie that Russia did it.

Many officials in Russia, such as Foreign Minister Sergey Lavrov, Foreign Ministry spokeswoman Maria

Zakharova, and Sergey Naryshkin, the head of foreign intelligence,

all raised the question of *cui bono*, asking who has the capacity and motive to do this. It all points to British intelligence. This operation—and this was pointed out by many experts and commentators—parallels what the British did in the Iraq case in 2003.

At that time, MI6 produced a dossier that supposedly proved that Saddam Hussein was in the possession of weapons of mass destruction that could reach any city around the globe within 45 minutes, and that Saddam Hussein had connections with al-Qaeda, a claim that was a blatant lie. Saddam Hussein had been locking up the al-Qaeda terrorists. But that dossier was then used as a pretext. Secretary of State Colin Powell gave his infamous speech in the United Nations motivating U.S. participation in the Iraq War. Then, the war against Iraq occurred, with many hundreds of thousands of people losing their lives as a result.

This is what some people in Russia are calling "Goebbels" propaganda. Why is there such a demonization of Russia? Why is there a demonization of President Putin coming essentially from the same people who are also demonizing President Trump and President Xi Jinping? This is the same foolishness which led to the Second World War, and which could easily trigger a Third World War. There is an imminent danger that these war-mongers will repeat the same methodologically stupid mistake which led to two world wars.

The Collapse of the Anglo-Dutch Empire

What is motivating this war-mongering is the desperation of the financial powers of the City of London and their Wall Street backers and collaborators, who see clearly that their system is failing. They fear that this could lead to a complete loss of their political and financial power. But they are also obsessed with the idea that their schemes will ultimately work, and if only they had just enough containment and escalation, then their system will be proven superior. They are confronted with their system not succeeding, but failing.

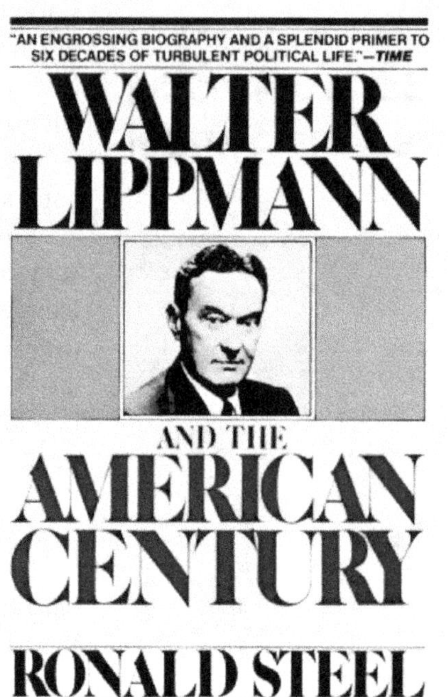

They don't have their intended unipolar world, but are instead confronted with the emergence of a completely New Paradigm in the world.

If you want to understand why Russia is such a focus,— of Russophobia right now, you have to go back to the time of the end of the Soviet Union. At the point when the Soviet Union started to disintegrate, the possibility existed for a peaceful world order for the 21st Century.

However, the consolidation of the neocons led to the revival of the American Century doctrine, which originally was formulated by Walter Lippmann in 1943. He published a book with that name, which then became the basis for the post-war order: the legitimacy of NATO and the Cold War. It was the idea to revive that with the project for a new American Century and the idea that you would replace the two superpower system with a unipolar world based on the Anglo-American special relationship, and a neo-liberal monetarist system. This was essentially a continuation of the idea that you would control the developing countries, keep them in relative backwardness, and deregulate the financial system in order to bring back the power of Wall Street and the City of London, and control the world that way.

In 1989, when Germany was reunified, reunification was combined with the promise that NATO would never expand eastward. You have to remember that the Soviet Union agreed to the dissolution of the German Democratic Republic and to German reunification without the use of force. You could say, in light of the history of the Second World War—in which the people of the Soviet Union suffered tremendous loss of life and still have a very terrible memory of Nazi Germany—that it was extremely generous of the Soviet Union to agree to it. The promise was clearly given not to expand NATO eastward; this was emphasized many times by the former American ambassador in Moscow at that time, John Matlock. In recent publications from the archives of George Washington University, it was also clear that this promise was, indeed, made.

Jack Matlock, Jr.

Manfred Wörner, Secretary General of NATO.

Promises Not Kept

In 1990, the Secretary General of NATO at that time, Manfred Wörner, made a speech in Brussels which is worth remembering. At that time he said, "The goal for the next decade is the creation of a European security structure, including the Soviet Union and the states of the Warsaw Pact," and that the Soviet Union would play an important role in the construction of such a security system, and that he could understand the wish of the Soviet Union not to be excluded from Europe. "The West cannot answer to the erosion of the Warsaw Pact with a weakening or dissolution of [NATO]," and therefore, "the only answer is the creation of a security framework which includes both alliances" and which brings the "Soviet Union into a cooperating Europe…. The very fact that we are ready not to deploy NATO troops beyond the territory of the Federal Republic [of Germany] gives the Soviet Union firm security guarantees," Wörner said.

This is all proven by the new documents that have been published. The neocons and their British partners were clearly promoting a different policy and making false promises. On the surface, the offer to the Soviet

Tony Blair

Union continued. Still in 1994, President Clinton said the NATO expansion is not anti-Russian; it means inclusion instead of exclusion. But then, things became more dramatic.

In 1999, there was the famous Tony Blair speech in Chicago. He called for the definite elimination of whatever relic of the Peace of Westphalia system existed; and by that, also the elimination of the principles of the UN Charter, namely, guaranteeing the sovereignty of every country. This was clearly a foreshadowing of what Blair did later in 2003 to ignite the Iraq War. The idea of "humanitarian" interventions replaced the idea of respect for the sovereignty of countries. Then in 2001, the September 11 attack was a complete assault on all civil liberties and civil rights which had been fought for, for decades. And it imposed an international regime with the pretext of the war against terrorism.

Regime Change Is Imperial Aggression

The policies that followed were regime change and color revolution. You had the Orange Revolution in 2004 in Ukraine; you had the Rose Revolution in Georgia. In the meantime, both the Russian and Chinese militaries respectively stated that they regarded color revolution as a form of warfare. The Maidan coup against the Ukraine government belongs in this chain.

In 2002, the United States had unilaterally abandoned the Anti-Ballistic Missile (ABM) Treaty, and proceeded to build up a global ABM system. Russia immediately said it could not tolerate Phase 3 and Phase 4 of this plan to be implemented, because it would completely undermine strategic stability and would therefore be a threat to the security interests of Russia.

In the 16 years of Bush, Jr.

Chinese financed and built high speed rail in Kenya.

and Obama, these interventionist wars continued. Bush declared the existence of an "Axis of Evil," and the various wars in the Middle East and northern Africa started to eliminate governments which were not agreeable to this idea of a unipolar world. The world was slowly and steadily going deeper into Hell, with more refugee crises, more misery, and millions of people dying in the Middle East and northern Africa.

2013: A New Option for Mankind

Then, in 2013, the world suddenly changed for the better. President Xi Jinping announced a new model of international relationships in Kazakhstan: He announced the New Silk Road, in the tradition of the ancient Silk Road, which was an incredible exchange not only of goods, technologies, cultures, and ideas, but also laid the foundation for a dialogue among nations. This New Silk Road undertook a development that is unprecedented, I think, in all of history. In the last four-and-a-half years, this new Spirit of the New Silk Road has started to catch on, so that now more than 140 countries are cooperating in Asia, in Latin America, in Africa, even in Europe, with the New Silk Road.

You have a tremendous sense of optimism in Latin America, where practically all Latin American countries are now building and planning to build bi-oceanic projects; a bi-oceanic railway between Brazil and Peru, bi-oceanic tunnels between Argentina and Chile, and many other projects. So, the Spirit of the New Silk Road has definitely caught on in the Caribbean and Latin American countries. It is certainly the case in the Asian countries, and many corridors are being built. Africa has completely changed with the building of railways from Djibouti to Addis Ababa, all along the eastern African countries, the western African countries. If you look at the map of Chinese investments in railway systems and industry parks and hydropower and many other, agricultural projects, there is a completely new spirit and self confidence among the Africa nations that they can now overcome poverty and under-development for the first time, in the near future.

The New Silk Road Spirit has even caught on in Europe, despite the efforts of the the EU to block cooperation with China. The 16+1 Eastern and Central European countries and the Balkan countries are actively part of the New Silk Road. Italy is now engaged, together with China, in a major project called Transaqua, which will change the lives of the people in 12 African nations and bring industrialization into the heart of Africa. But also, Portugal and Spain want to be hubs, not only for the western end of the Eurasian part of the New Silk Road, but to be also a hub for the Spanish- and Portuguese-speaking countries in Africa and Asia and Latin America. Switzerland, Austria, and even Holland, Belgium, and some of the Scandinavian countries are now, early in the game, seeking cooperation with China. So, the New Silk Road Spirit is on the agenda.

Win-Win Cooperation— The Three Presidents

It is based on the idea of win-win cooperation, of respect for the sovereignty of other countries, and respect for other countries' social systems. This has been an incredible development. It's already twelve times larger than the Marshall Plan was, but the amazing thing is that during the last four-and-a-half years of enormous progress in this project, the Western mainstream media and Western politicians have virtually ignored it; they have not reported it. Only in the recent period have they suddenly realized it is unstoppable. What is now occurring is a flood of attacks from the main think tanks, saying this is just an authoritarian effort by the Chinese to replace the Anglo-American imperialism with a Chinese one, and that China wants to take over the world. It was quite a sudden change in the coverage and in the comments.

They got a similar shock when they realized that Russia was not merely a regional power, as Obama had claimed, but that it was about to become, under the leadership of President Putin, a major power again. So therefore, when Trump suddenly won the election, the same apparatus that is now behind the Skripal affair—British intelligence in collusion with the intelligence heads of the Obama Administration—started a policy of a coup against President Trump.

There was an article in January 2017 in the British magazine, *The Spectator*, which said that President Trump would be gotten out of the White House through a coup, impeachment, or an assassination attempt. That was the policy which these people followed, and the aim

Urs Lustenberger, President of the Swiss Asian Chamber of Commerce.

clearly was to prevent President Trump—who had promised in the election campaign to improve relations with Russia and restore relations to a stable, positive basis— from doing so. His opponents basically said: "If you dare to speak to President Putin, that just proves you are a Russian agent." In fact, it took until the G-20 meeting in Hamburg last year, before Putin and Trump had a personal meeting, during which they hit it off very well.

Trump Wants Good Relations with China and Russia

President Trump and President Xi Jinping also got along very well in their first meetings, despite China-bashing language from Trump during the 2016 election campaign. President Trump received President Xi Jinping in April last year at his private residence in Mar-a-Lago. They established a very good, positive relationship. Then, when President Trump went to Beijing for a visit in October last year, President Xi Jinping returned this welcome, and gave Trump what China called a "state visit plus." President Xi Jinping had the Forbidden City closed down to visitors for an entire day, and gave a long lecture on Chinese history to President Trump and his wife. They established and deepened their relationship.

In the meantime, Russia and China also established the deepest strategic partnership in their history. Putin gave a speech on March 3, 2018 to the Federal Assembly, in which he announced new weapons systems, including a long-range missile which does not follow the ballistic curve, but is highly maneuverable. Then also, a nuclear-powered cruise missile which the West does not have, and a nuclear-powered underwater drone which is quicker than above-water ships, and, in addition, laser weapons. The combination of these and other weapons means that all of sudden, the entire global ABM system the United States had proceeded to build is obsolete.

President Putin noted that the West had refused to even respond to all the offers to negotiate made by Russia since 2002, but now, they have to respond. It is quite amazing that, except for the demand of four American ambassadors, the West has not yet responded. Western media have tended to belittle these new weapons systems, or ignore them for the most part.

Chinese Foreign Minister Wang Yi and the Chinese Defense Minister Wei Fenghe have just attended the very large Seventh Moscow International Security Conference, which was attended by 900 guests and 700 media. Wang Yi said that Russia can pursue its own interests and play a larger role on the international and regional stages. Chinese Defense Minister Wei Fenghe said he came in order to send a signal to Washington that the Russian-Chinese alliance is the strongest and that there is a very close cooperation between the Russian and the Chinese armed forces.

All of these things have to be seen as a dynamic process. We are now also on the verge of a full-fledged trade war. Admittedly, the trade deficit the United States has with China is untenable.

China and the U.S.A. Can Work Together

But when President Trump said that he wants to impose tariffs first on $60 billion of Chinese imports, and then on another $100 billion of Chinese goods, this was met by an unusually sharp response from the Chinese. *Global Times* wrote yesterday that China will not submit to U.S. trade intimidation; that China is prepared to react with a full list of its own tariffs on American imports; that the trade war will cause pain for China, but Chinese society will rally and unite around the government and the Party; and that they will also present a detailed plan to respond, and then Americans will have to choose whether they back their President's actions, or whether they hold him accountable for the consequences. *China Daily* even mentioned that the Chinese countermeasures could include the dumping of U.S. Treasuries, of which they have $1.4 trillion.

All of this comes at a moment at which, at any moment, we could have a new financial crash much

President Trump (left) greeting President Putin at the APEC Summit, November 2017.

worse than that of 2008, because all of the central banks have done nothing to remove the root causes of the 2008 crisis. They just did quantitative easing, zero interest rates, and many corporations took that gratis money to buy back their own stocks, so that their stock exchange values would go up, but the corporate debt would increase. Now, as the Federal Reserve is trying to increase the interest rate, the blow-out of these corporate debt situations could trigger a complete systemic collapse. That is just one of the many facets of this crisis.

An insider in the banking system, a well-placed one, told us very recently that it is possible that some of the financial forces would deliberately trigger a crash, which they know is inevitably coming, to pull the rug out from under President Trump, so as to bring back the neocons, and in that way solve the problem which they did not solve with the failed Russiagate coup attempt. One thing is very clear. If that were to happen and the neocons were to fully return to power in the United States, World War III would be certain.

In the middle of this Skripal affair, President Trump and President Putin talked by telephone. President Trump refused to send out tweets on this affair or otherwise join in the present Russia bashing.

I want to make the strong point that there is a solution to all of the problems I have just mentioned. That is, that there are many possibilities. For example, when Presidents Trump and Putin have a summit in the near future, they could discuss this. Also, the Chinese Prime Minister, Li Keqiang, has recently pointed to the fact that there is another way to solve the trade deficit, namely, by massively increasing mutual trade. Presi-

Xinhua/Lan Hongguang

China President Xi Jinping (R), meeting U.S. President Donald Trump in Mar-a-Lago, Florida, April 6, 2017.

dent Xi Jinping has offered cooperation with the Belt and Road Initiative to the whole world, including all the European nations and the United States. China could decide not to dump U.S. Treasuries as a punishment for the U.S. trade measures, but they could instead invest the $1.4 trillion in U.S. Treasuries in infrastructure in the United States.

The U.S.A. Needs U.S. Methods with China's Participation

Diane Sare mentioned the Manhattan subway system in her introductory remarks, and if you look at the infrastructure—not only in Manhattan, but in all of the United States—the condition of the highways, the absolute absence of a high-speed rail system, it is very clear that the United States urgently needs investment in infrastructure. President Trump had promised in the election campaign that he would invest $1 trillion in infrastructure build-up, but so far, he has not been able to find any financing, because the private investors want an 11% to 12% return and a complete return of their capital within 10 years. Which means it is not possible to finance it through private investment. The neocons in the Senate and in the Congress do not want to spend it from the Federal budget. The idea to distribute the cost to the regional and state governments is just not practical.

If, on the other hand, China—which has a fantastic high-speed rail system of, I think, 25,000 km of high-speed rail, and is planning to connect every major Chinese city with a high-speed rail system and have 40,000 km of high-speed rail systems by 2020,— if China could help to build such a high-speed rail system in the United States and connect every major city with a 350 mph high-speed rail system, and in that way, completely transform the infrastructure of the United States, it would not only help to overcome the trade deficit, but would open the way for joint ventures between the United States and China in third countries, such as in Latin America where, contrary to what former Secretary of State Tillerson had said, China is not trying to build an imperial system. Instead, China and the United States could join hands in building up the industries of the Southern Hemisphere.

Also, the same could happen in Asian countries along the Belt and Road, and also in Africa. It could happen in the reconstruction and economic build-up of the war-torn region of Southwest Asia.

This could even include Great Britain eventually, if it changes its government and if it clears up the crimes it has committed. But it absolutely requires the reform of the financial system of the United States and Western Europe.

Lyndon LaRouche's Four Laws

My husband, Lyndon LaRouche, several years ago developed a policy package which would remedy the situation: The United States should go back to its original Hamiltonian banking policy, to a banking system in the tradition of Alexander Hamilton, including the Glass-Steagall banking separation introduced by Franklin D Roosevelt. The package requires a national bank, a national credit system, and a crash program for thermonuclear fusion and joint space cooperation with other countries in order to increase the productivity of the economy in a qualitative way.

What people really don't realize, or most people don't realize, is that the present Chinese model of economy and the early U.S. republic model are very similar. They're based on Hamiltonian principles.

In China, they have now made a huge effort to eliminate the speculative area, to forbid Chinese investors abroad to invest in speculation. It is very clear that China—even if it doesn't call it by that name—is very close to the American System. And it is no coincidence that the most popular economist in China is Friedrich List, the German economist who in a way was the predecessor of Henry C. Carey, and who wrote important works about the difference between the British and the American systems. Germany also has such a tradition, namely, the *Kreditanstalt für Wiederaufbau*, the Credit Bank for Reconstruction, which was based on Roosevelt's Reconstruction Finance Corporation and was the basis for the German economic miracle in the postwar reconstruction. So, also in Europe, you have some relevance and memory of this system.

Now after Xi Jinping announced the New Silk Road, the *Executive Intelligence Review* and the Schiller Institute published a study that we had been working on for 26 years, *The New Silk Road Becomes the World Land-Bridge*, which is a full blueprint and outline for the international economic cooperation of all nations to overcome geopolitics.

Moralize the American People

Just imagine if we could mobilize the American people to exert pressure on President Trump and give him the backing he needs. He would be able to accept the offer of Xi Jinping to cooperate with the New Silk Road. Then the European countries would have no choice but to eventually recognize,— most of them are doing it already, but even the remaining ones would recognize that cooperation with Russia, with China and other nations that have already joined the Belt and Road initiative, that this would be much more in their self-interest, than the present course of the British confrontation with Russia and China.

If such an international economic cooperation could be realized, it would also be the realistic basis for a global security architecture that would include, among others, Russia and China. It would then require that we do exactly what Xi Jinping has said many times: Mankind needs to move to a new phase of international cooperation, what he calls the "shared community of the future of mankind" or a "community of common destiny." Then we could start to focus on the real problems, the common aims of mankind. We could build a system to make nuclear weapons obsolete, a new form of the Strategic Defense Initiative (SDI), which my husband proposed at the end of the 1970s. It had been in the works for several years, and then on March 23, 1983, President Reagan announced the SDI as a way for both superpowers to cooperate to make nuclear weapons obsolete.

I think in light of the present danger of a new arms race and the already-existing arms race, and the danger that it could get out of control, we need such an approach as a new SDI, and also a new Strategic Defense of the Earth (SDE), because the planet as a whole is threatened by dangers from space, from asteroids, and from comets that could extinguish all life on this Earth.

Common Aims of Mankind

We should instead concentrate on the common aims of mankind—the alleviation of poverty, the creation of a living standard for a decent life for every human being on this planet, and a system of earthquake precursor detectors and joint space research and travel. We should concentrate on space colonization as the necessary and possible next phase of the evolution of the human species. I think that if we combine that with a dialogue of cultures, in which each nation would emphasize and revive the best traditions of its own culture, and then have a dialogue among all of these nations and cultures, we could create the basis for a new Renaissance.

Skeptics would say that this is completely unrealistic. But I'm saying that the fact that you have these three presidents—President Putin, who is recognized and loved by the Russian people, and has just been re-elected with an overwhelming majority; Xi Jinping, who is an exceptional leader who is equally loved by the Chinese population— they decided to eliminate the limits to his term in office so that he can guide China in these very, very important coming years; and President Trump, who is absolutely not what the media makes of him. He has shown again and again that he has outflanked a quite difficult factional situation in his own party, and a Congress that stands as an obstruction for the most part.

If the three presidents join hands and do what they have clearly done very successfully so far in the attempt to solve the crisis of the Korean Peninsula, this is a realistic option.

However, we should not sit on our hands. We should launch an international mobilization to propose this agenda, and do everything in our means to make it possible. The life of civilization depends on it.

Thank you.

There Can Be No Justice Through Violence

These greetings from Ramasimong Phillip Tsokolibane of the LaRouche-South Africa Movement, were presented to the Schiller Institute Conference, "A Dialogue of Three Presidencies: Bending the Arc of the Moral Universe Toward Justice," which was held in New York City, April 7, 2018.

From Africa's leading nation and proud member of the BRICS alliance, the Republic of South Africa, I greet you who are assembled today in New York City and around the world. I address you as a leader of the LaRouche movement, but also as a South African patriot and participant in the events that led to my country's remarkably peaceful transition from a savagely brutal, racist regime—whose inhuman apartheid policies rightfully received global condemnation—to an imperfect but perfecting republic, in which all of our citizens have an opportunity to live as human beings, in the pursuit of progress and happiness.

Our nation has always drawn a particular hatred from the British Empire and its lackeys. They have never forgiven us for their defeat in Anglo-Boer War in 1902. It was the British oligarchs, with their evil and inhuman Royal Family, who have tirelessly sought to sabotage our freedom; it was these British who have manipulated the uninformed and the stupid, pitting white against black and black against white; it was the British who were the true authors of apartheid, even as some among their own leaders offered sophistic criticism of the white victims of their manipulations.

If the truth be told, racism and murderous policies to eliminate Africans—white and black—have been and remain mainline British imperial policy. "Race science" is a reflection of the outlook of the British Empire, and was promoted by leading British imperialists long before they created the Nazis to preach and enforce such evil. When His Royal Virus, Prince Philip, the moldering male concubine of the Bitch Queen, speaks of murdering billions, in order to purge the planet of its human "overpopulation" that "threatens the wildlife"—the same wildlife his fellows feel no compunction about hunting down and killing— I know that he is speaking of me and my fellow Africans.

As we discuss today the legacy of that great American, Martin Luther King, Jr., we must always remember that we can never defeat evil by using the methods of evil. We can never gain a new and better world by drowning the old world in the blood of our enemies. Justice for everyone, including those who Dr. King referred to as "the least," cannot be the product of violence. We must fight on a higher level, as did Dr. King, using love, creativity, and non-violence as our method, as we stand for our principles that lead to true revolutionary change. We must be willing to give up our lives in defense of those principles.

I consider myself such a revolutionary, as do—or

Dr. Martin Luther King, Jr.
(1929-1968)

should—all members of our movement. The changes we seek are an overturning of the Brutish Empire's global system of economic slavery. I am not a pacifist, but a warrior fighting in the way that Dr. King fought for change and justice, through creative non-violence.

What do I mean by "creative non-violence"? Consider the work of the father of my country, Nelson Mandela. Mandela never met Dr. King, although they were kindred spirits, committed to justice and against all forms of racism. Our father was not a violent man, but he was a fighter nonetheless, who, like Dr. King, reflectively struggled to find the center of his own humanity. Like Dr. King, Mandela steered a movement that was constantly under violent attack, and which included many people, even in leadership positions, who advocated violence against the brutality unleashed against them.

Nelson Mandela
(1918-2013)

In his twenty-seven long years in prison and isolation, our father came to understand, that while such violence might *appear* to be self-defensive and even justified, given the brutality of the apartheid system and those who enforced it, violence would only lead to a bloodbath, a slaughter of his people and the whites, who were, after all, mere pawns in the larger British game, that pitted peoples and even nations against each other, for the benefit of British imperial interests.

Our father therefore, prior to his exit from prison, conceived of a completely different strategy, which to almost everyone but himself was considered impossible: He would turn his enemy into his ally, by appealing for peace, and truth and reconciliation. As he was fond of saying, "Everything seems impossible until it is done." Nelson Mandela turned his erstwhile enemy, State President F.W. de Klerk, into a co-advocate for the peaceful transformation of South Africa into a nation ruled by blacks and whites *together,* by appealing to de Klerk's better self. In that way, the British Empire's plan for a race war in South Africa

that could have spread throughout Africa—fulfilling His Royal Virus' desire for depopulation—was defeated.

Established in 1995, the Truth and Reconciliation Commission gave an open airing to at least some of the crimes and injustice of apartheid, clearing the air for a black majority government and our current Republic. Truth and reconciliation is still a work in progress, made possible by Mandela and his fight to accomplish peacefully what was considered impossible.

And is that not what Lyndon and Helga LaRouche have done, as well? Go back more than thirty years. Who, especially in positions of leadership, envisioned then the global revolution in progress today, in which the leaderships of Russia and China are co-operating to create a new paradigm of global economic progress, with the offer and possibility that a maverick and unexpected U.S. President, Donald Trump, might lead your republic to join with its former "enemies" in this effort? The LaRouches not only saw this as necessary and possible; they worked to make it the reality it is today. This gives the British Empire and the deranged Royals nightmares. It is precisely this New Paradigm which is fulfilling that promise and hope for a non-violent revolution for a better world for which Dr. King gave his life, and which was the lifelong ambition of our father, Nelson Mandela.

I am proud to be part of this revolution. The British Empire and what it represents is not defeated yet, but I say to you, with great conviction, that the defeat of that British Empire is coming, if we stay committed to our principles and our belief that love and creativity triumph over violence and evil. Together, we will overcome!

Thank you, and best wishes for the success of your conference.

Ramasimong Phillip Tsokolibane
April 5, 2018

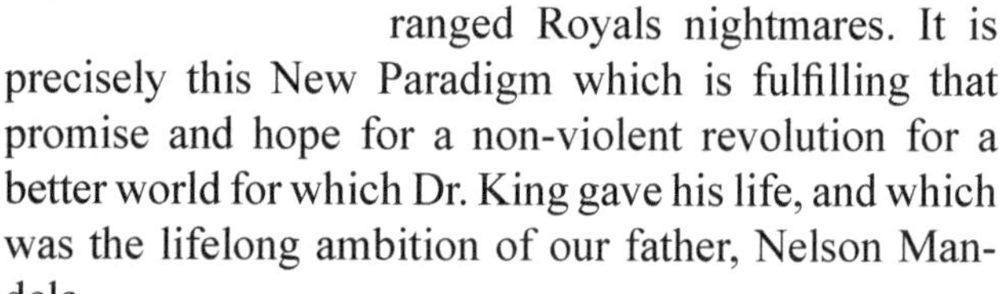

May 8, 2014

EXTENDED REMARKS & FACTS:

Economists Who Were Usually Stupid

by Lyndon H. LaRouche, Jr.

Notably, references made here, must begin with these following, necessarily, multiply extended, prefatory remarks. These are made respecting those matters, which will be shown, below, as having been lodged within what are now, in effect, matters subsumed under a necessarily, somewhat extended history of my own early, formal, education, as follows:

My Extended Education

I was born in Rochester, New Hampshire, on September 8, 1922. My own education since I had left a Rochester school at the age of ten, had moved me into a Lynn, Massachusetts grammar school in 1932. That had scarcely been much of a success, as ordinary matters go. Many among the teachings supplied by the Lynn, Massachusetts schools in my own time there, had often been filled out with the relegation of the subject of mathematics and its derivatives, to what is presently traceable to the then wicked influence of Bertrand Russell. That had been an influence which had been felt approximately world-wide, by the time of the end of World War I.

In my experience, there had been some exceptions to a more general incompetence of education in schools; but, those exceptions had been limited to a relatively few classes from among the total. I came to see this more clearly, in my concluding three years at Lynn English High School, which were, otherwise, virtually a total disaster, as, similarly, my later experience during the nominal university education administered to me in a university in Boston and its vicinity, before and after military service in the U.S.A. and, then, Asia after the close of World War II.

The best feature of any competent report on my educational experience, is, still, today, that it was, frankly, the more disgusting as several years had passed.

The Worst Characteristics

The worst characteristics which had been common to the classes in education, were those in Lynn, Massachusetts, first, and, later, Boston. In both of the two cases, the relevant worst effects were the most disgusting with respect to a practice of a body of teaching which had been based on the defense of Euclidean geometry, and its derived expressions, such as the depraved mathematics which had been premised on those fraudulently adopted presumptions which had taken control over trans-Atlantic education, at the beginning of the Twentieth Century, in place of actual science.

EIRNS/Claudio Celani

"Watching the Teachers Enter." Lyndon LaRouche writes about the failures of public education when he was a student, some 80 years ago, but since the death of President Kennedy, the quality of education has declined even more precipitously.

This fraudulent substitution is to be witnessed, still today, since the 1900-dated campaigns of David Hilbert, in France in 1900 A.D., and, slightly later, the outrightly Satanic influence of Britain's Bertrand Russell world-wide: that consolidated the beginning of the early 1920s, ever since, up to the present time.

The relatively worst cases of the post-Nineteenth Century's moral and intellectual degeneration in education, generally still worse presently, have been typical of the destructive force of moral disaster, which is quickly identifiable as "reductionism:" a worsening pathology, which had, then, already permeated the educational systems in both secondary and university-bases. This wicked change had been premised upon merely an essentially linear, actually anti-

scientific hoax: virtually, an avowedly mandatory hoax, resting on the farcical teachings which were commonly based on the neo-archaic root of an *a-priori,* Euclidean geometry, and on the related offshoots of a mere arithmetic, not an actually physical science.

This was a mere arithmetic which had been installed as a proposed replacement for actual science, and which has remained as increasingly hegemonic throughout both the Twentieth Century, and also the early Twenty-First this far. Those trends of degeneration in educational and merely allegedly scientific practices, and their effects, have remained relatively hegemonic, although entirely fraudulent, and, also, as systemically opposed, fiercely, to any semblance of an actually physical, modern science.

By my time in life, that particular fraud, of Euclidean geometry, had generally saturated the pores of the system in that High School which I had attended in Lynn, Massachusetts, then, in particular, and continues in an actually worse form presently. That factor, was systemically destructive in its effects on the most among the students there, and was, also, visibly damaging to potentially cognitive powers of the students, more generally.

At Lynn English High School

What had saved me from much of this corruption, in particular, went according to the proverbially Scottish references to the notion of "all that," as having been the interventions, by competent leading elements of the Lynn, Massachusetts directors for the city's educational system, notably senior official Stephens and the head of the Lynn English High School.

There, I was justly rescued, initially, by the results of my simply taking an "I.Q." test, which proved to me (and relevant others), sufficiently then, to be startlingly clear evidence, initially, against the vicious abuses generally practiced, in particular, in the Eighth Grade of school in which I had been virtually pilloried at that time, by the abuse by some of the faculty of the relevant Junior High School, where I had been subjected to such treatment, prior to the taking of that standard "I.Q." test of the time. It was the result of that test, which had prompted the higher ranks of the Lynn school system, to liberate me from the vicious abuse to which I had been subjected by that so-called Junior High School Eighth Grade.

The resulting evidence shown then, and later, was that I had been an exceptional talent. For that reason, I became, soon, a bit later, once more, the victim of a new source for a virtual intellectual "lynch mob" hostility against me personally, which had included a large ration among some of the faculty of the Lynn English High School at this time. The sponsors of that sort of "pogrom," were those teachers of the type who had preferred that the students not actually think too carefully, but, rather, should simply attempt to repeat what they had been taught by the combined efforts of teachers and by the texts supplied.

Thus, what had happened in the 8th grade experience, appeared, afresh, as widely echoed among the faculty at the Lynn English High School. There were some exceptions to such "popular abuses,"[1] particularly among the better scholars, but the ugliness remained the prevalent truth to be spoken respecting the prevalent practice throughout the general environment, there.

The "I.Q." tests which I had experienced, both in the 8th grade case, and, freshly in the Lynn English High School, had each demonstrated a relatively exceptional, so-called "I.Q.," rating, for which only a relatively very small minority of the students were qualified. Unfortunately, the connections to those abuses to which I had been subjected in the Eighth Grade, were not limited to that school; they had been, essentially, the same stupid abuse which would, and did cross-infect a relatively large ration of even the Lynn English High School faculty (with some notable exceptions), within the Lynn school system. The later, second, "I.Q. test," showed evidence of suggested higher achievement levels, with respect to those which had

been measured earlier, for the Eighth Grade affair.

There was, nonetheless, a continuing targeting of students who were, not only even merely, "quicker learners;" but, actually original thinkers, a type which were emphatically not wanted by certain, unfortunately prevalent, malicious clusters, assembled from among the faculties in both Lynn and, later, my experience with relevant Boston university educational programs. Some of the faculty are to be blamed in those cases; but, like, the administration of the Eighth Grade, and the later class-work at the High School levels, they were, generally, intellectual disasters in fact: both for the students, and the effects shown in the shaping of their judgments in later years.

Only in few cases, over the full course of that time, those who stood out as valuable exceptions, especially in the non-mathematical aspects of the education, showed their significant resistance to the more popular follies; but they were, nonetheless, only a relative minority. When the faculties were corrupted in that respect, they had been, for the most part, also, even vicious in protecting their often dubious expressions of appeals to an allegedly "popular opinion" of "those regular guys and girls" who were, generally, more concerned with being considered as "popular," than seeking the merits of their future roles in society.

The results of what I have already referenced here, as the twice-repeated I.Q. testing of me, had seemed to have virtually saved my need to sort out good, or, at the least, merely decency, from the intellectual "lynch-mob" sort of bestiality preponderant in the general educational environment. My "I.Q." testings by the educational departments, had occurred on two most notable, relatively successive occasions; these tests had shown me, as also the relevant officials, exceptionally high qualities of competence in my own performances, as shared among the relatively upper ranks of intellectual development within the student bodies during those times. The most notable effect of this testing, was, for me, the importance of seeking to re-enforce what had been tested as indications of my own, relatively superior notion of truth, generally; this would be con-

---

1. I must admit, that the almost regular, weekly beatings I enjoyed from my mercurially disposed, from "enraged to publicly charming" father, were an aggravating consideration in the process as a whole; but, the one factor only re-enforced the other. The only effective resolution, was to rely on my own stubborn commitment to the notion that only the truth of a matter was a satisfactory resolution.

tinued by me, as a pattern, as from the close of my secondary education into some dismal university years.[2]

My personal experience on this account was never unique in and of itself. The technically identified practice of talking-down students in public schools into a state of moral confusion, and, similarly, also in universities, has been, now increasingly, a generally accelerated practice of presently current educational institutions, which was a cause for an increased moral and intellectual degeneracy-rate which has been increasingly acute since the assassinations of President John F. Kennedy and his brother Robert, and since the parallel spread of drug-addiction among soldiers and others during the interval of the U.S. part in the worse than useless Indo-China war, as both President John F. Kennedy and General Douglas MacArthur had forewarned, prior to the assassination of John F. Kennedy, and as during the closely following death of our republic's then greatest living military strategist, Douglas MacArthur.

The alleged, chiefly fraudulent "Case of Lyndon LaRouche," has thus continued to reflect what has recently been the usual quality and effect of what I experienced in the setting of the educational systems, of my own knowledge; but, at the same time, it expressed, more importantly, a characteristically declining intellectual quality of the educational, and functionally related institutions, over the course of the passage of recent decades, a moral and intellectual decline which I had already experienced, since my experience with what I have indicated as educational processes, up through the present time. It is, notably much worse, presently, especially among the adolescents, and younger, than ever before. However, the typical sophistry practiced publicly by typical members of the Congress, for example, shows too much of a similarly regret-

Capricho 37: "Might not the pupil know more?" Francisco de Goya (1797-98).

table performance in respect to the need for truth expressed in the public interest. The decadence of the standards of judgment by the U.S. Congress, has been the fruit of two leading factors: the declining quality of intellectual competence in the U.S. government itself, especially since the assassinations of President John F. Kennedy and his brother, Robert, coincided with the plunge into a British-directed, important increase of relative stupidity within nearly all categories of the general population since the assassinations of the two Kennedy brothers, and the rise of the politically induced, virtually decorticating "Green" intellectual pestilence, which

---

2. Although there had been a useful purpose in the "I.Q." tests, their merit was, nonetheless, a matter of estimated relative accomplishments, according to roughly clear and distinct categories; but, they were otherwise matters of pragmatically useful assortments of relative categories, which served as meaningful notions of a series of categories, not an absolute measure.

has been increasingly prevalent throughout most of the dope-soaked ranks of such increasing rations of the mentally and morally incompetent of the increasing rations of the dope-soaked sector and related, "green" brain-drained, and the increasing ration of the often wobbly-headed sections of the U.S. population presently.

Into My University Years

My own university years, had been, essentially, a morally dismal aspect of public and related education. I have recalled it, as, being often begun on a much lower level of the intention of education, than had been the case in the Lynn, Massachusetts high school system. The education of the particular university life which I had experienced, was predominantly below the quality of the education which I had received, earlier, in the Lynn High School. The passage from the President Franklin Roosevelt/World War II generation, into the post-Roosevelt, relative moral and intellectual degeneracy of the Harry S Truman Administration, was directed, via Wall Street, by the Truman-Churchill-Bertrand Russell "Witch-hunt" trend, a trend which had produced an induced, long-ranging decline in the moral and intellectual qualities of performance of the U.S. population generally, even in virtually all relevant categories, moral categories, most emphatically.[3]

My second experience with that same Boston-area University on which my father had repeatedly insisted, had credible exceptions such as an academic year's study in "the German language for us seeking careers involving chemistry," or a smattering of the principles of chemistry in some of the faculty, or, also the literary skills of a certain Dean of the university, and some intermittent, useful snatches of chemistry caught between-times. Otherwise, the experience there, was an exposure to a chronic sort of pedagogical disaster which had rather simply reflected the influence of the Twentieth Century's fraudulent, but also decaying dogmas of relying on merely mathematics, rather than actually physical science, while tending, either to avoid all actual science, in favor of eliminating the influence of actual science, or, to craft a mere appearance of a glib showing of some of "the real stuff."

Certainly, not all among the professors and instructors, were actually incompetent; but, from the moment of the death of President Franklin D. Roosevelt, the culture of the United States, was already in precipitous decline under the freshly accelerated pressures from the British empire's increasingly over-reaching control of the post-FDR United States, chiefly, then, under the dictatorship of Winston Churchill and, more importantly, the virtual Satan of almost the entirety of the Twentieth Century, Satan's clearly own Bertrand Russell. Such were the exemplary effects which had fostered the predominant spirit of increasingly decadent sophistries permeating the atmosphere of the institution of education itself; this effect was both the principal source and medium of the practiced intellectual, and also moral corruption, if sometimes, even with a mere taint of competence to "so to speak," lend a mere appearance of the poorly refined coating placed upon the correspondingly disgusting cake. The prevalent rule was, of the customarily and monotonously corrupt, "go along to get along" mentality: a spirit of "sham" which has permeated the life of our institutions, not excluding the U.S. Congress, generally up to about the present time.

Somewhat Later:

During that same period, but following the close of World War II, I had returned to the university which I had suffered through earlier, but I had sometimes enjoyed encounters with some eminently important professional physical scientists, and the like, met from the context of such as the Harvard environment. At that time, I was one among those with whom I had recently returned from the concluding term of my military service in Asia; and, I had enjoyed the degree of confidence which I had brought back with me from the latter phase of that military experience abroad; but, I had also had more than enough of the university to which I had mistakenly returned, briefly, after military service. All-in-all, this was a tasteless experience which I briefly endured only for reason of the pressures from

---

3. I treat this delicate subject, in appropriately selected, later chapters following.

New York State/Library of Congress

LaRouche's wartime service, like that of other veterans, meant that they "were no longer children to be taught; we preferred to be those who selected their destiny as a matter of a maturing personal judgment respecting the necessities for the future." Here, returning troops express their jubilation at returning home, Aug. 6, 1945.

my father. However, his pressure on that subject had lost any further meaning for me as a dweller in the post-war world: I set forth, thence, to seek out, and make my own future, thenceforth. The pathway leading up, was chiefly rugged; but, it was not long before the appropriate remedy appeared; now, I had excelled within the scope of my professional assignments, until the FBI moved in to spoil matters for a time.

Many among us, notably from my own post-war generation, reacted similarly to my own reactions, in the respect, that being "away to war-time service," had marked out an interval of lapsed time between entering and leaving military service. That circumstance, had, thus, tended to separate our pre-war outlook on society, from our post-war sense of personal morale, and morality, alike, from an experience of an adult identity under the resonant leadership of President Franklin Roosevelt.

For me, this resonance was potently emphatic. This effect included my often justly contemptuous attitudes toward the "kid stuff" aspects of university life: we, of many veterans among my generation, were no longer children

to be taught; we preferred to be those who selected their destiny as a matter of a maturing personal judgment respecting the necessities for the future. We may have been denied that goal, from case to case at hand, but our intention was for scientific, economic, and cultural progress.[4] In the meantime, under Truman and the continuing "witch-hunt" moods even under President Eisenhower's Presidency, the pressures reflected the heavy hands of the notorious Dulles brothers, as we had known this fact during the course of World War II itself.

The single most notable implication of the aforesaid experience with both secondary, and higher education at the relevant institutions of learning, is that my intellectual achievements in later adult life, as in Lynn, Massachusetts' I.Q. examinations, were, in performance, among those in range of the standard of the 125-148-score level denoted by the relatively different standards of the Academic and Military-service ratings: obviously, merely approaching the "genius" sectors, if not reaching it; but, nonetheless, thus approaching the relatively highest ranking professional competence attained during my many later decades of my profession as a physical economist in the domain of real life within our nation and abroad.[5] The

---

4. "Old dogs," with whom I might be classed today, tend to have that spirit which I share presently on this account. Some among our generation's sons and daughters are prone to respond to that spirit which resides as if within a resonance somewhere in our bones. The "I.Q." issue associated with my undergraduate and later development, is highly relevant with respect to the two upper strata of the relatively senior generations, much more so than citizens now in their twenties, or their parent's generation. The quality of both those latter, a generation later, have been, generally much poorer in education and in economic and cultural opportunities, than my own immediately junior generation of the approximately fifty-to-seventy-year-old batches, or those presently living still older, if they are still economically and culturally active.

5. A "physical economist," is efficiently defined as one devoted to those principles of physical chemistry chosen for purposes of economic practice, rather than the foolish babble of statistical mathematics. Science is a matter of achieving the future realities unknown to the mere past and present, as even the most modest appreciation of the principles of chem-

actual problem was to be located within the social system of so-called "Popular Opinion."

The Standard for Meeting Achievement

The root of those defects has lain, clearly, within the characteristics of a relatively declining quality of so-called "public opinion," an effect which tends to determine that the younger generations will be, since the end of the 1960s, less intelligent in actual practice, than those of the older. This, somehow, despite the true genius of the founders of modern European (and, hence, also American) intellectual achievements in modern science and Classical artistic performance, who are best gauged, practically, as by the standard of the leadership in the actual founding of all competent modern science, such as that under the leadership of such as the actual, trio of original founders of modern science, in order of sequence: (1) Filippo Brunelleschi; (2) Cardinal Nicholas of Cusa; and, (3) the unique achievement of Johannes Kepler of the original discovering of the existence of the Solar system.

Later, there were the foundations laid by the Winthrops and Mathers of Seventeenth Century Massachusetts, or their successors, such as Cotton Mather, in particular, who fostered the great genius and founder of the American Revolution, Benjamin Franklin, and such singularly great geniuses as our General Alexander Hamilton (the true founder of the economic system of the original U.S. Federal Constitution).

The physical science founded by Brunelleschi, Cusa, and Kepler, situated the progress effected by such outstanding figures, such as the true giants of the Seventeenth and early Eighteenth centuries, as Carl F. Gauss had been followed by his most brilliant student, Bernhard Riemann. Riemann made the revolution in science which the great Max Planck and Albert Einstein had later defined, respectively: the new minimum (Max Planck), the new maximum for science (Albert Einstein); and then, as being the successor for Kepler's earlier role in Renais-

sance triad: the great Russian-Ukrainian, Vladimir Ivanovich Vernadsky, whose work in the foundations of physical science, had achieved a higher meaning for insight into man's relationship to the Solar system as such, than ever before: the unique, astrophysical efficient principle: the essential function of ontological advances in human life, as a basis for existence within the Solar system (and beyond) *per se.*

Education Since Franklin Roosevelt

Afterwards, the assassinations of President John F. Kennedy and his brother Robert, were combined with the effects of the wretchedly wicked venture into the graveyards of souls, which had even more than destroyed human bodies in the lunacy of the U.S. launching of its War in Indo-China, a war which was merely another holocaust of wasted lives set into motion by the influence of the British empire under the influence of the frankly Satanic Bertrand Russell.

The concomitants of all this, for me, had been, that since the testing which had led to my "double promotion" from the Eighth Grade, I had come to understand, increasingly, on successive points in what was for me, the history of my reflections: the specific failures of the educational processes to which I had been subjected, and which I had sometimes bitterly resisted, as in my public schools' and in the aborted quality of most aspects of university education. This became more, and more clearly understandable as time had passed.

Post-World War II times and their developments since the time of the death of President Franklin D. Roosevelt, confronted me with the essential lesson-in-life: to become fully aware, in retrospect, of my own intellectual vindication on precisely that account: an achievement largely embodied in a deepening of a sense of a necessary distance from what had been, chiefly, a past into which I had come to know I had been dumped, in the main.

In fact, it had become, and remains the fact that my intellectual development in respect to these matters of education, had been far above the level of virtually all my known contemporaries, not only in both secondary schools and my later experience of then-customary university indoctrination. That has been the case ever since, as continued through the present time: but that also in the matter of the proper principles of statecraft.

My particular hatred, today, on this account, has been against the mis-teaching of science, a practice which has been premised on the basis of merely mathematics as such, as in the present tradition of David Hilbert and Bertrand Russell. This means that we must, urgently, end the fraud typified, by such cases as the stubborn hoax of Euclidean geometry, which persists, in the guise of Hilbert and Russell, as the most effective instrument of evil against humanity since Zeus and Satan themselves. My sharpest and most bitter insight into the root-cause for my own hatred of that wretched sort of education which I had, largely experienced: it presents a reflection of my confrontations with the post-World War II doctrines of the British Empire's leading professional Satan of the Twentieth Century, the same Bertrand Russell, himself.

My Own Profession

Today, my initial, and still-current profession, has been that of employment as a specialist in economic forecasting, a role which had begun during the late 1940s, and, soon-thereafter, as a secondary executive in the same consulting firm. Those few years in practice in that position, were, first a consultant in the field, and, then, a secondary executive official of the same firm's executive.[6]

Nevertheless, during that lapse of time. I had already become among our nation's leading economic forecasters, in the middle to late 1950s, and since, now, about now sixty years ago, and still presently. My rise to first-rate status in actual achievements in forecasting, had initially spanned an interval of time, from the time of my 1968-1971 forecast of the profound, coming crisis of the U.S. economy, whose result has been, since, a continuing, downward trend in the physical aspects of the U.S. economy, an economy which has continued to plummet since then, up through the present date at the brink of a general "bail-in" collapse of the trans-Atlantic region of the planet.

I attribute my success as traceable, originally, to the impact on me of such as, most notably, originally, that of such as the Gottfried Leibniz, who had been the inspiration for the Eighteenth-century American Revolution, especially under the role of Benjamin Franklin, and the founding of modern economic science as such, by the memory of the British-assassinated, Major-General Alexander Hamilton's systemic perfection of his design for the four founding principles of the U.S. economy, principles which remain as the only actually competent founding principles of a science of physical economy throughout the entirety of the world of today.

The truth of that success of Hamilton's special genius, has lain within the bounds of the actual distinction of the human species, its distinction as superior to all otherwise presently known expressions of life, as, also, not so incidentally, tied to the greatest chemist of modern life, Russia's greatest modern scientist, Vladimir Ivanovich Vernadsky: the superb scientific genius who had actually discovered the distinctive principle of human life with such remarkable precision, and insight into the meaning of that life within, explicitly, the presently known bounds of the Solar system.[7]

---

6. In fact, this experience had provided me with a solidly successful position in professional economic performance: which had been continued until I had inadvertently crossed swords with the FBI. As was more or less a custom for such encounters, the FBI's wrath produced a divorce from my enraged first wife, a divorce, thus, arranged by an "old family friend," who had assured her, most emphatically, that all of this had nothing to do with the FBI as such. Nevertheless, during the meantime, I had already become our nation's most successful economic forecaster, that beginning the timely outcome of my widely publicized, timely forecast of the probable crisis of the U.S. financial system for within the interval of 1968-71: just in time for the major crisis of 1971-1972. My part in that forecast event had then been prominently featured internationally, in conjunction with a famous defeat of the British spokesman whom I had defeated in a celebrated international conference, held at Queens College, New York City. Nevertheless, during the meantime, I had already become, in fact, among our nation's successful forecasters, from during the middle to late 1950s, already, now sixty years ago, and still presently. My rise to first-rate status on this account, now sixty years ago, had initially spanned an interval of lapsed time, from my 1968-71 forecast of the profound, coming crisis of the U.S. economy which since, then, has been a continuing, downward physical-economic

trend in physical aspects of the U.S. economy, an economic trend which has been, since then, continued to the present date, where it hangs at the brink of a threatened "bail-in" collapse for the trans-Atlantic system.

7. The case of the systemic achievements of V.I. Vernadsky is the subject of the concluding chapter of this report.

EIRNS

LaRouche attributes his sucess as an economic forecaster to the impact on him of, among others, Gottfried Leibniz, "the inspiration for the American Revolution, especially under the role of Benjamin Franklin," and Alexander Hamilton's American System economics. LaRouche is picture here with this famous "Triple Curve Function," 2003.

I. The Roots of Modern Science As Such

Presently, I continue to trace the actual foundations of modern science back to what is named as "The Golden Renaissance," since no later than the Fourteenth Century. This had been a most profoundly revolutionary turn, upward, into all achievements of modern history, and has been the sources of the actual quality of human mental modern progress typified, by that origin, as by the leading contributions, precisely, in turn, for principle, in the already cited threefold succession of Filippo Brunelleschi *(the physical principle of the ontological minimum)*; Cardinal Nicholas of Cusa *(the physical principle of the ontological maximum)*; and, then, Johannes Kepler, the principal follower of Nicholas of Cusa, thereafter, and of the originally modern discovery of the categorical concept of the existence of the Solar system, as such, by Johannes Kepler.

The triad of the work of those three founders of the original modern European civilization, were coherently related, as founders of all competent modern science. They had lain the foundations for the subsequent genius of such later, exemplary modern geniuses, as Gottfried Leibniz, Carl F. Gauss, Bernhard Riemann, Max Planck, and Albert Einstein. However, from that point in time, on, as during the same time as the work of Planck and Einstein, and times beyond since today, the notion of the very meaning of even the mere name of science, had since been first polluted, and then virtually destroyed: that done, most notably, by those two figures who became prominent for their own specific crimes against science and humanity, alike, since the dates of the period beginning the year A.D. 1900: these were the dates of the foolish figure of David Hilbert in Paris, and, a short time later, Hilbert's frankly Satanic follower, Bertrand Russell.

The common feature of the dogma of both of these latter two cases of Twentieth-century corruption, Hilbert and Russell, had produced a presently continued, generally accelerating, degeneration of the practices of both science and economy, a pollution with the after-effects reaching (formally) from the onset of the Twentieth Century, to the now increasingly threatened general cultural and economic collapse of trans-Atlantic social culture, presently. This has been, a decline which has strictly dominated the United States of America, in particular, since the deaths of, respectively, U.S. Presidents Franklin Delano Roosevelt, and President Roosevelt's implicit echoes, President John F. Kennedy and his brother Robert.[8]

Since the assassinations of President John F. Kennedy and his brother Robert,[9] the economy of the trans-

8. The period of transition, into the modern crisis of the Twentieth though the Twenty-first centuries, so far, had actually occurred during the last decade of the Nineteenth Century. It had been the British Royal Family's ouster of Germany's Chancellor Otto von Bismarck, soon followed by the assassination of France's President Carnot, which had been the opening of the transition to a permanent state of global warfare (with temporary vacations) from the ouster of Bismarck, through to the present state of thermonuclearly threatened world-wide thermonuclear warfare.
9. And, also, implicitly, the related, attempted assassination of President Ronald Reagan. Most of the assassinations of U.S. Presidents, and similar notables, have been effectively identified as having been traced to British Empire operations. Not coincidentally, the victims were usually from among the best Presidents, or Presidential candidates, as I have pointed out crucially significant cases of such coincidences. I have compiled a relevant review of the entire roster of our Presidents, heretofore, with relevant evidence as to correlatives.

Atlantic region of the planet, has been careening in an, overall, generally downward direction, a continuing process to be located, more narrowly, in the 1968-1971 turnabout into a generally downward, now continuing physical collapse of the immediately trans-Atlantic economies, *per capita*. All allegedly subsequent, actually net economic growth of the United States has fallen, in net effect, as a presently accelerating rate of downward-turning, and still accelerating downward, physical-economic trend, since that time, up to the present date, and, still being extended, prospectively, into the immediate future beyond. This has been, and presently remains a condition immediately threatening a prevalently accelerating collapse-rate of the U.S. economy, which has been accelerated, economically and morally, alike, at increasing speeds of collapse since the succession of the "Junior Bush"-Dick Cheney Administration, and Obama's willful collapsing of the U.S. human economy, all done under an actually British imperial dictatorship over the United States, and our plunging Presidencies, our Congress in the main, all that plunging downward, at accelerating rates, most emphatically, since the close of the William Clinton Presidency, through to this present moment.

The Continuing Downward Trend in U.S. Society

How far beyond will this downward plunge now go?

That will depend upon the arrival of appropriate measures for any possible recovery of the trans-Atlantic economy. That means, in turn: that, at this moment, the probable survival of both peace and the U.S.A. alike, depends on the urgently required, immediate expulsion, for much urgently justified cause, of President Barack Obama. Although the U.S. Presidency, must, nonetheless keep Obama safely alive, even if in the prison which he deserves for his crimes, the security of the United States, and avoidance of thermonuclear warfare, requires that he had been placed, safely, out of the harm's way of both the U.S. Presidency, and that the U.S. citizens of the present and future, would never make the present kind of the same mistake, or its likeness, ever again.

I have recently set forth, in earlier publications, the most indispensable of those U.S. political-economic reforms, which, in particular, should be sufficient to bring about a sudden and intrinsically successful, reversal of the presently downward-plunging economies of both the Americas and of western and central Europe. These

would be, specifically, the principles of economy of the great American geniuses in economics such as Benjamin Franklin, General Alexander Hamilton, and such specific followers of Hamilton as the Presidents Abraham Lincoln, William McKinley, Franklin D. Roosevelt, and John F. Kennedy, but, also, including, actually useful, recent Presidents of good intentions and skills in their own persons, such as, recently, Republican Ronald Reagan and Democrat William Clinton (no Bushes included). Since then, there has been a worsening of the recently worse-than-useless Presidencies. The actual (i.e. net physical) economy of the United States, since the assassination of President John F. Kennedy, has been driven in a net downward trend-line motion, in fact, since the beginning of the 1970s.[10]

All of the habituated trends in U.S. policy-directions have been, overall, disasters not to be perpetuated; they have all been cardinal disasters for the United States, and, above all, for our population at large.

Our National Intellectual Sickness

The downward trend of the physical economy, *per capita*, is to be measured, essentially, not in money, but presently accelerating degrees of collapse in physical economy, together with the deterioration of intellectual capabilities, and of the physical conditions of life and culture of the population generally. These have been, generally, downwards intellectually, and with respect to public health, with each succeeding new generation of predominantly incompetent, addictions-ridden adolescents and younger ages, alike, presently.

For example, the promotion of the spread of a mind-busting national drug-recreation-habit and, unfortunately, correlated intrinsically fraudulent cures, alike, has driven the present youthful and middle-aged population, down from the quality of a leading skilled work-force of the world, as in the time of President John F. Kennedy and Kennedy's most admirably productive contemporaries in our nation's leadership, into a relatively tiny minority portion of the post-adolescent and older, potentially useful work-force; but, worse, to a relatively incompetent, and pitiable unstable, relatively tiny fraction of the adult population as a whole. The fostering of the use of narcotic and related substances, and personal social practices designed for comparable effects, has produced the effect of a labor-force, chiefly without actually productive skills, or even a meager

---

10. The recently notable exceptions have been, most notably, President Ronald Reagan (of SDI fame) and peacemaker President William Clinton.

The worse-than-useless, vastly influential, and abominably super-wealthy, coexist alongside a weak-brained, ill-fed, utterly confused so-called "labor force," without significant skills, and rapidly vanishing options for continuing even mere subsistence.

level of economic and social competence. The abundantly worse-than-useless, vastly excessively influential, and abominably super-wealthy, seem to present us with a weak-brained, ill-fed, utterly confused so-called "labor force," mainly without significant skills, and also rapidly vanishing options for continuing even mere subsistence, all the while the greatest Wall Street hyperinflation in all modern history, crushes the remaining mass of the population under the weight of the unpayable debt of those who are the merely financially rich, but the worst than useless for the needs of mankind presently.

A sweeping correction of those ills accumulated during and since the war which John F. Kennedy and General Douglas MacArthur had forbidden, is urgently needed, as an immediate reform, if our nation is to survive at all. In brief, Europe generally, and the Americas, too, have fallen into the same trap of evil, a cult of Zeus-Satan worship, exemplified presently by that quasi-global, British imperial monarchy, which has been modelled upon the proximate precedent of the, frankly, inherently Satanic Roman Empire.

The predators of trans-Atlantic region, are worse than useless speculators, sucking, intellectually and financially, on the proceeds of Wall Street and those related monetarist speculations, which have dominated and looted the economies of the trans-Atlantic economy, that done ever-more vividly, as a presently downward-accelerating trend, since the onset of the term of office of President Richard Nixon: the falsely, merely apparent (if only to the duped), net gains have always been merely nominal; the far more important, physical trends, have always been downward, if in more or less degree, during the passage of lapsed time since the close of the U.S.A.'s 1960s.

Why the U.S. Economy Has Plunged Downward

All progress by living processes, has been, and remains, premised upon the intrinsically needed rise in the interrelated sets of productive capabilities of mixed groups of living species, the human species, far above all. Progress on this account, is always expressed as in net effect, an upwardly evolutionary process of human cultural development into higher relative levels of per-capita energy-flux densities (as measurable in terms of reference to human chemistries/energy-flux densities of per capita, productive practice), excepting for exceptional, planetary catastrophes. The only exception to that requirement, is the human species, which increases its role among living species only voluntarily, rather than by simply biological interactions among species of plant, animal, etc., or, as by interactions among the set.

Only the human will is an exception to the rule, that all animal species otherwise, each, animal or vegetable, progress merely as a species, and that, implicitly only temporarily, except by a humanly determined influence on them: as V.I. Vernadsky has produced the evidence for this view of the relations respectively distinguishing the human species' upward self-evolution absolutely superior to both inferior living species, and to those human populations which resist their indispensably upward accelerating, physical-economical progress per-capita, upon which the continued existence of the human species itself, ultimately depends. This gain is a feature of the demonstration of the exceptional case of mankind: mankind as embodying the living processes of the uniquely human creative actions, which distinguish the human species, from all other living species otherwise known to us.

This power of the human will, depends upon a biologically evolutionary process, one which is integrally not only bio-chemical but willful. The specificity of the uniquely human property of the noëtic will is the ability and determination to continue to rise to ever higher developments achieved, in the fruitful realization of upward progress by means of ever-higher per-capita energy-flux densities of useful action, which is the most essential distinction of the human species' successful abilities, against all supposed animal alternative forms of life. Precisely that, is the most essential expression of the human will, known, essentially, as expressed, historically by the voluntary employment of the necessary use of fire as the "fuel" of the human species' willfully voluntary rise to ever higher orders of usefully expressed increases of the relative energy-flux density of the efficiently per-capita powers of the membership of the human species.

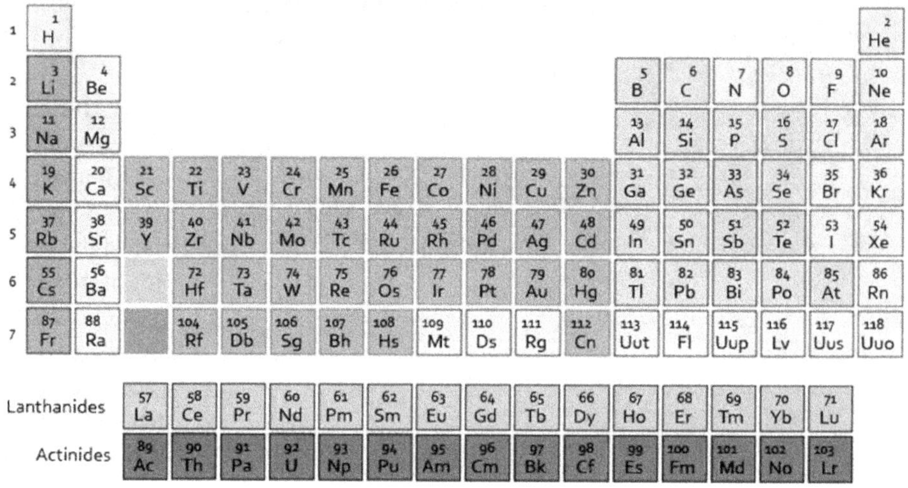

Man's Enemies: Zeus, Satan & the British Empire

The measure of that humanly voluntary increase of the energy-flux density of the human will, per capita and per unit of energy-flux density, is expressed in the notion of the famous *Promethean Principle*, as opposed to the currently "Green," Satanic-Zeusian principle embodied in both the myths of worship of the oligarchical pestilences known, interchangeably as the wicked systems of tyranny such as what has been known recently, as both the Roman and British empires.[11]

The presently clearest, and, also, exemplary, scientific account of the distinctions to be considered on this account, is located for chemistry by the physical development of a rate of increase of power of the human biologically, done through rises which correspond, in fair description for our purposes here: to the process of man's rising power of the role of chemistry, as measurable, in effect, in higher degrees of the power of the human species' unique option for the practicing of successively higher ranges of living chemistry.

For example: The Meaning of Modern Chemistry

Beginning with the Nineteenth-century process which had led into the Nineteenth Century's concluding decisions respecting the effects orderable in the mode which became known as physical chemistry, such as that of the famous Periodic Table. This occurred during the course of the Twentieth Century, when the "original Periodic Table" came to be recognized as an evolutionary process within the original framework of the Periodic Table, with the demonstrably evolutionary contributions

FIGURE 1

'Original' Periodic Table of Elements

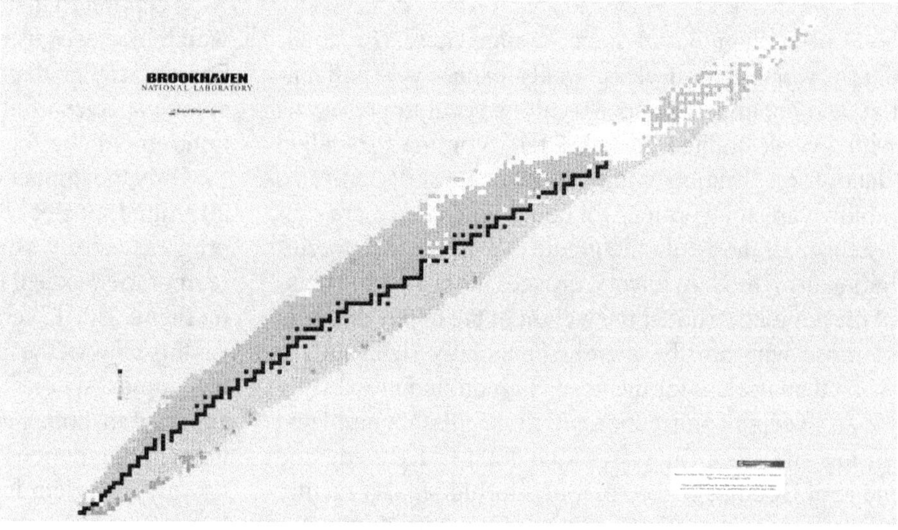

FIGURE 2

'New' Periodic Table: Nuclides

---

11. I.e., the "oligarchical principle" of the Zeus-Satan cultural formations. Rather than, for example, the Christian Apostolic Principle, which was always intrinsically Promethean when properly informed as to effect and intention: a dedication to the future mission of mankind's development through the uniquely noëtic powers specific to the human species, against the intrinsically Satanic, "green" ideologies.

to insight into a mankind-driven increase in the range of the so-called "elements" of the original conception of the periodic table as such, as shown by the study of the evolution into higher, synthetic powers of upward evolution, largely (for us presently) through elementarities beyond the original notions of radioactive chemistry: the higher energy-flux densities of the new chemistries produced within the range of the Twentieth Century and beyond, have been, and will be even far more advanced in adducible energy-flux ranges in densities of energy-flux densities, implicitly, at least potentially, than the indicated point-by-point potential of our Sun itself.

On this account, truly competent modern science, contrary to the pro-Satanic, "Green" dogma, has provided those who care, with appropriate insights into the implications of the work of the greatest modern exponent of human life as such, in the implications of the achievements of the most important modern scientist of life this far, V.I. Vernadsky. Today, the fact is, that mankind has achieved the demonstrable design, as this had been done by mankind ourselves, which reaches beyond the range of the energy-flux density of the expressed power of energy-flux densities, if only in detail, higher than those of the Sun as a whole, presently. That signifies, that mankind's present potential has reached, already, experimentally, inherently energy-flux densities beyond any otherwise presently known means within the known bounds of Johannes Kepler's uniquely effective discovery of the principled existence of the Solar system as such.

The consequent fact is, that the noëtic powers of the human mind will almost certainly come to exceed (implicitly) those known abilities of the Sun which are implicitly inferior to the implicitly promised, higher order of constructs and products of the practice of the human mind.

Mind: thus now signifies, that the powers of the human mind's continued, upward development in power of practice, pertain to an inherent characteristic of the human mind, as such, rather than the mere functions of the human brain as such. This distinction, which lies beyond the reach of all presently known experiences of mere human sense-perception, reflects a kind of power which excludes any merely animal life *per se*. It is a power which reaches far beyond the powers of human sense-perception, such that only man's progressively advancing process of creation of this effect, enables mankind to efficiently recognize those powers in the universe whose distinction is, that they exceed, implicitly, and also entirely, the bounds of relatively miserable,

original human experiences of mere sense-perception.

On that just-stated account, the particular case of the work of Vladimir I. Vernadsky, time itself is inferior to the specific talent of human creativity. This was the emphasis which he had reached in the course of the evidence of his work: man, thus, must create himself, upwardly going, in a direction of developments intending to seek endlessly ultimate relative perfection in the goals of human creative progress itself within that Solar space originally discovered by Johannes Kepler, and beyond. Thus, merely biology, as it had been customarily defined even among most merely technical scientists of our present time, had been a power qualitatively inferior to the characteristics specific to the actual potentials of the human mind, as the great scientists arisen from the Nineteenth and Twentieth centuries had done. Science in its right name and true nature, exists only beyond the wretched limits of merely human sense-perception: it lies in the effects which are to be recognized as beyond the reach of merely sense-perception as such, and beyond "whoever might have gone before us."

So, in such a circumstance, Eratosthenes' discovery of the magnitude of the Earth, was a relatively early kind of a masterful type of true knowledge, reaching beyond the meager means of mere human sense-perception, as a true science, gained from the observation of the true object of the image which the Sun of the Solar system casts upon Earth. It was an image, to be seen in the mirror defined for this purpose, as the footprint of the Sun which represents a truth beyond the pitiably silly presumptions of merely human sense-perception *per se*.

With that measure, which had reached to levels far superior to Archimedes's merely reductionist's abilities, mankind, is actually knowledgeable in a quality and degree, far beyond the reach of mere sense-perception: the principle of knowledge, had always departed the illusion of mere human sense-perception, into coming to actually know the Earth as far beyond the mere human personal sense-perception. Mankind continues to view the events on Earth as ontologically from far above mere sense-perception, as such. This must be done, now, from the minimax principle of Johannes Kepler's discovery of the Solar system, into the Galaxy and states of entities far above that, wherein the ever new truths about man, are now waiting to be discovered.

Such is the basis for the continuing development of mankind's knowledge of science into regions of knowledge far superior to mere human sense-perception as such: beyond all of the silly notions of mere sense-certainty *per se.*

Such, immediately above here, leads our attention into the more urgent considerations which I will now outline for you, below, as follows:

II. The Crucial Role of V.I. Vernadsky

In the meantime, during the still-living achievements of Russia's Vladimir Ivanovich Vernadsky,[12] the greatest scientific discoveries of universal principle have, so far, only been touched, while being, already, presently, the most crucial knowledge of physical science yet to be discovered: knowledge which relatively immediately, awaits us, but still unattended by most of even the seemingly best-informed human scientific minds.

In brief, V.I. Vernadsky was the original discoverer of the most important principle presently available to only the very best among modern physical science. There is no proper justification for tolerating the all-too prevalent, backward view of the current state of science-topical affairs. The subject which I now introduce immediately, does have, conveniently, certain characteristic appearances of a preliminary nature, which are qualified to prompt

"V.I. Vernadsky's fundamental discoveries in physical science live in the very foundations of the actual meaning of the human mind."

preliminary insights into the territory on which I am reporting here.

On this specific account, it would be incompetence, for me to neglect taking into account my own knowledge respecting the distinction between the Soviet Union as a reflection of the scientific and artistic culture of Russia prior to the Bolshevik Revolution, and the complexities inherent in the evolutionary social process of the Soviet Union's infiltration by, chiefly elements recruited, such as the British dupe, A.I. Oparin, into the

---

12. Aka: V.I. Vernadsky.

process, by the corruption of British intelligence operations linked to the inherently Satanic Bertrand Russell, as that is now to be considered with respect to the conditions since the influence of the initially British establishment of the installation of the Adolf Hitler regime. Consider this matter, in the following terms:

The Franklin D. Roosevelt Factor Cuts In

It is commonly said among decent people, that President Franklin D. Roosevelt was a true genius, whose passion had done wonders, the like of which, no other person of the Twentieth Century had matched. Indeed, much of the "secret" of President Franklin Roosevelt's works of true genius, was manifest only after his recovery-inspired inspiration, as expressed as his miraculous upward surge of his intellectual creativity had, itself, lived long enough to inspire, also, such as the John F. Kennedy inspired by widow Eleanor Roosevelt, and John's own brother, Robert. V.I. Vernadsky would have implicitly agreed with such an outlook, and that is not merely as an adornment.

Such considerations engage a profound principle of our universe (at least for as much as scientists generally know as both the Solar system and defeating the hazards of the journeys through the tracks of the Galaxy which contains it). V.I. Vernadsky's virtually miraculous mind, touches upon such higher ranges of matters located within particularly important celestial processes. Such is the human mind's potential, which actually dwells within that domain, which we are, currently, usually left more to admire than to manage; but, notwithstanding all commonplaces, V.I. Vernadsky has been the greatest well-known scientist in respect to his actually accomplished and still living achievements, this far. If you think differently, it is clear than you must have missed the most important, presently knowable, scientific facts.

This is not merely justified praise of his accomplishments; there is a much more profound issue to be considered, and that very seriously, all for pressing practical reasons, on this account.

Against the background of the immediately preceding paragraphs, above, there is a second general observation, which complements a related, also crucially important, subject matter, a matter on which V.I. Vernadsky's fundamental discoveries in physical science, live in the very foundations of the actual meaning of the human mind. I identify that point as a first consideration, as a key point for this part of the report.

Summarily: the central achievement of the great scientist called Vladimir Ivanovich Vernadsky's principles of universal scientific practice, can be located in his demand for the discarding of the claims to the meager existence of the notion of an independent principle of *time per se*. The creative powers of mankind, rather than time as such, are the essential metric of mankind's achievement of knowledge of the universe: the truly fundamental scientific principle of practice is that of the actual "clock to be kept," the imagined clock of the ontologically willfully anti-entropic progress of the human species, as opposed to belief in objects floating within the opinions of those less articulate scientists who define themselves, foolishly, as being located within a merely imagined physical space and time. In fact, the most essential parameters, so employed, are, relatively speaking, one very big "boo-boo," that of overlooking of essential and otherwise well known, factual evidence: there is much too much reliance on the intellectual quicksands of belief in mere sense-perception *per se.*

Consider the merely apparent controversy which my own immediate remarks here might, mistakenly, presume, as if, out of the scientific ignorance expressed as believing in a physical space-time premised upon a merely notional principle of the functions of merely *space-time matter.* They may admire the idea of science, as that may be properly said: but, actually, they have the principles of that which are only ostensibly scientific: which is to say belief in reality "bass-ackwards." Rather, as V.I. Vernadsky stated his point with both the utmost clarity and scientific truth, as well: it is mankind's own existence, as V.I. Vernadsky also argues, which actually measures the superior, if seemingly only some more powerful shadow-like attributes of mankind's actually determining existence of a really living, uniquely human species: as a force within not only the future history of mankind, but a reflection of the true law of the universe, from the top, down, not the bottom-up.

Man may be imperfectly educated, if otherwise skilled; but, the imperfectly practicing professional scientists, tend toward what should be an obviously mistaken presumption of their belief in falsely premised, essentially crucial omissions of regard for the essentially inclusive, most crucial, actually experimental facts in available evidence. There are several crucial, higher categories involved: which we must take into account as interlocking categories of the systemically erroneous, but also commonplace, ontological presumptions.

The essential blunder, which even almost every scientifically respectable professional, usually, makes, up to recently known date, is the plausible, but, more correctly named also stupid presumption, that mankind's existence is, *a-priori*: which is to claim that man is situated within the context of the mere reductionist's silly notion of physical space-time. Admittedly, the false presumption, in other words, is the presumption that life, as such, is, itself, a product of the reductionist's imagined notion of an axiomatically, mathematical-physical space-time: a belief, or merely a set of presumptions, which is to be counted, essentially, as just another kind of example of the malicious idiocies of the Twentieth Century's foolish David Hilbert, and, of the relatively contemporary, and frankly Satanic, Bertrand Russell, and the latter's like.[13]

The origin of the commonplace fallacy which I treat here, is best attributed to the adoption of a certain blinded faith, to the effect, of an axiomatic presumption of the essentially mythical blind faith in a presumed functional quality of "elementarity" attributed to human sense-perception *per se: a delusion which had been already discredited by the importantly discovered principle of Eratosthenes' measurement of the Earth. It is the delusion of belief in a sense-perceptual phenomenon of human sense-perception, as lying within the domain of sense-perception of an object within the atmosphere of Earth, as compared to the* transit of the cycle of the observation of the position of the Sun lying

---

13. This is, by no means, even a slight exaggeration. It is largely a folly to be blamed on the conditioning of students in their classrooms, or related circumstances, which prompts them to rely on taught-down teachings of the classrooms and related circumstances. Their teachers, textbooks, classrooms, popular opinions, and so on have taught them down into swallowing it, as prevalently acceptable presumptions in the mode of commonplace matters of mere opinion, whether gained from passing quips of the classroom, or similarly reckless modes of defining of so-called, merely popular opinion.

outside the imagined atmosphere of human sense-perception.

It is, as a matter of principle, that, the experience of the humanly attributed rotation and displacement of the relative position of the Sun, were an ironical matter, respecting an irony essentially unknown until the triad of the combined notions of the minimum principle of Filippo Brunelleschi, the maximum of Nicholas of Cusa (without elementary linear characteristics) and the third, essential part of the essential conception: the principle expressed in Johannes Kepler's discovery of the inherent principle of motion within the identity of the Solar system, which exists only without, rather than merely within.

This is to be compared with the viciously reductionist error inherent in the presumptions of the otherwise very clever and energetic Archimedes. It is, ultimately, the universe itself, which is actually elementary as a process: just as life *per se* can not be the product of a reductionist phenomenon. In fact, it is a true universal principle of the universe, that the particular phenomenon can only be a fruit of the relatively encompassing universality, as Carl F. Gauss carefully avoided telling what he had known in the circumstances posed (indirectly to him) by young Bolyai, and the latter's own father.[14] The time was not ripe for him to say certain things he knew very well; he had wisely, and certainly implicitly, trusted the future accomplishments of his brilliant protégé, Bernhard Riemann, then, on the occasion, presenting a great work, Riemann's historic Habilitation Dissertation, presented in the honoring of his great mentor, Carl F. Gauss.

Discussion:

What had struck my attention, on this account, had been, that since the British empire had used the death of President Franklin D. Roosevelt as the opportunity to continue World War II under a commitment to a nuclear conflict with the Soviet Union, and a reign of terror inside the U.S.A. itself, all under the virtually terrorist reign of the foolish Harry S Truman: which had left the Soviet Union itself with an internal division of notability, between those who adhered to their connections with the British Empire, as Bertrand Russell's worse-than-Nazi trained, intellectual dupe, the typical reductionist of Russell pedigree, such as A.I. Oparin, versus the actually scientific cultural outlook of V.I. Vernadsky, who has been, since his death in 1945, a crucial, available instrument of modern science for the fostering of the rescue of the world from the nightmares which the British Empire's Bertrand Russell had foisted as an evil, upon a post-President Franklin Roosevelt's heritage, up through the times of a number of the presently ongoing, Federal incumbencies since the administration of President Franklin Roosevelt, in particular.

The crucial fact, respecting U.S. laws' insolent evasions of the U.S. Federal Constitution, has been the increasing rate of a general lack of actual principle, by the great majority of former Presidents of the United States: a majority which had made way for the production of particular laws which were, then, and are, now, inherently violations of the underlying intention of principle for the Federal Constitution. Treasury Secretary Alexander Hamilton was assassinated, by the British Empire's agent, Aaron Burr, to protect the corruption of the U.S. Constitution, in the name of "States Rights," the "States Rights" fraud against the U.S. Constitution, supported by some Presidents such as, early on, John Adams, Thomas Jefferson, and James Madison. U.S. Presidents Monroe and John Quincy Adams, had restored the United States to its Constitutional intention, in repudiating the errors of Adams, Jefferson, and Madison.

The professional British assassin, Aaron Burr had financed the British imposition of the introduction of the British interest against the United States, executed by the criminal figures of Andrew Jackson and Martin Van Buren; and, there was no effective President from that time, until the President Abraham Lincoln, whose leadership had saved the United States.

Naturally the British empire, personally, had organized, from operations launched in Canada, the assassination of President Abraham Lincoln and other British targets in the U.S. during the same time.

These historical facts, respecting the United States' government and its history, bear essentially on nations such as Russia today, still, because the United States, which had been created to serve as an instrument for spreading human freedom throughout the world, had been so often turned by the British empire and its Wall Street money-maker elements, into either a simply

---

14. See: C.F. Gauss to F. Bolyai, from Göttingen: June 3, 1832: the work of the great mind of Gauss himself, presented to ease the tension expressed by Farkas Bolyai, the father, respecting the subject presented by the son, Janos Bolyai. Carl Friedrich Gauss: **"Der Fürst der Mathematikers" in Briefen und Gresprächen.** Kurt R. Biermann, Verlag C.H. Beck, Munich, 1990. An interesting posture by Gauss, in dealing with the passions of the father and son respecting the inherent evil of Euclidean geometry.

powerless U.S. national leadership, or an utterly corrupted one, by the influence of the British imperial interests globally. Vernadsky's contributions to all humanity's benefit, were in the process of being realized through the role of President Franklin Roosevelt, during the relevant moment of world history; the death of that President followed, who would have, otherwise, saved the planet from the prospect of new world wars, which has ensued since, through the British Empire's control over the U.S. Government, through the accession of the inherently disgusting, puppet of Winston Churchill, and, more significantly, the truly Satanic figure of pure evil, world-war-maker and mass murderer otherwise, Bertrand Russell.

Consider thus, the submission of Presidents to the powers of the British agents known collectively as Wall Street; the root of these evils has been the lack of an actual notion of physical principle, a deficiency which was made way for, by the British-like substitution of merely current shifts in proximate opinion as an unprincipled notion of matters bearing on Constitutional law: beginning with the case of the intentional fraud against the Federal Constitution known as "States Rights," and the international implications of using a "States Rights" basis, as was done in the State of Virginia, against the actual intention of the Federal Constitution, as was done by such Presidents as John Adams, Thomas Jefferson, and James Madison: the "loophole in the Federal Constitution" through which herds of British elephants might have marched (and often did) without effective obstruction: a mere confederation of states, intentionally circumventing the Federal Constitution, as Adams, Jefferson, and Madison, had done, as had Jefferson in abandoning his office under President George Washington—while professional British assassins such as Aaron Burr could have created the evil, openly and explicitly, which would become the skunks Andrew Jackson and Martin Van Buren. Profiting against the United States, is a practice which leans toward treason against the most precious principles of our Republic.[15]

The very meaning of United States of America, under the design of its Federal Constitution, had been that the states are subjects of the Constitution of the United States, and are obliged to conduct their foreign trade accordingly. Hamilton's assassination, as the greatest economist of the original United States, since the death of Benjamin Franklin, has been, as Treasurer, and also a Major-General, the leading representative of the design for the U.S. economy, who had created the world's greatest economic-policy design in world history so far, was assassinated by the British imperial interest. The great evil to be destroyed, on this account, still today, is the failure to recognize that the mere money of any actually sovereign nation has no intrinsic value, other than the trade in physical values within itself, or in uniquely physically actual traffic among others.[16] Only such precautions can assure the actual sovereignty of any individual national republic, if it expresses, more or less perfectly, its truly efficient sovereignty, free from submission to foreign powers and their agencies. In short, Wall Street, and its like, must neatly and summarily, be put out of existence, for reason of the continuing, systemic existential fraud.[17]

The relevant implication for that argument by me in this present report, is that the wisdom of nations, in practice, can only be expressed globally in one of two ways: either agreements in human economic policies echoing the original American settlements on behalf of freedom for all peoples, but, that including such essentially historical predecessors as the great Renaissance's Brunelleschi, Cardinal Nicholas of Cusa, and their essential representative Johannes Kepler, with his unique discovery of the Solar system and its underlying scientific principle. However, the contemporary realization of that intention depends presently, upon a very specific role of the great-

---

15. Notably, money as such has no honorable principle. It is merely a means of exchange, honorable only as a charge against the sovereign nation-state which has uttered its currency; that is key for understanding what has corrupted our United States' Government increasingly, as with the inherent corruption of substituting money-as-such for the same physical principles of progress which inhere in the practices, respecting the use of money, by the four fundamental rules of Treasury Secretary Alexander Hamilton, on which the foundations of the economy of the republic of the United States had depended. Anything contrary to that principle, is and would be a fraud against the principle on which the United States was created. All true economic value is intrinsically physical, not monetary, as Treasury Secretary Alexander Hamilton had defined the relevant notion of national currency used as a means for exchange, within the nation, or, in other currencies, by other nations, for physical goods in fact.

16. E.g., value under the standard of V.I. Vernadsky's principle of intrinsically human value.

17. This means, as I have stressed earlier, that there must be a transformation of the U.S. national banking system, conducted under the authority of the Secretary of the Treasury, which bans all banking, excepting national banking, by national executive authority of the Treasury *per se*. Federal decrees and related decisions under Federal regulation are to be applied accordingly.

est scientist, in effect, who has been, so far, V.I. Vernadsky's discovery of the living meaning of the human species in both past, and present universal history.

The Very Crucial Implications: The Options

The crucial importance of Russia at this moment, lies in the implications of the continuation of the relatively unique scientific legacy of V.I. Vernadsky, for both Russians and large sectors from among the Ukrainians: the true, presently living spirit of national unity of elements of Russo-Ukrainian culture when considered in its history as representing a basis for a Eurasian unity in economic and related practice. The best hope for the planet as a whole, at this juncture, will be, virtually uniquely, a Eurasian alliance of its own, most able, and best with the United States itself. Only consider the implications of the wonderful potential of emphasis on leaps forward in thermonuclear fusion's role in increasing the level of applied energy-flux density to a mankind, still on our planet, but reaching out from Earth to bring a needed, humanly directed development into, initially nearby regions of Solar space, through robotic systems controlled from Earth, but, nonetheless gaining a power within the Solar system itself, which are a source of the power needed to maintain the Sun as viable factor in the protection and development of the Solar system, and of the challenges which accelerated leaps higher, scientifically, within the Solar system, will make feasible for our humble living-space back here, on Earth. For example: NASA restored and amplified for its role as an increasingly potent and effective planetary factor within, and ultimately beyond the mere Solar system itself.

With the termination of institutions such as the pro-Satanic cases of the Roman Empire and the present British empire, the historically imperialist systems of ancient and present times, must vanish from the practices of the planet, immediately. The careers of the likes of the Zeus and Satan, such as the Roman and British empires, must be brought to submission to a cooperative order among the sovereign republics, who must now triumph over the, actually pro-Satanic, oligarchicalist imperial tradition, such as the present British empire. Let the nations choose their independent identities, as President Franklin D. Roosevelt had intended for as long as he had remained alive: the means by which the progressive future of mankind, throughout, and beyond this planet, must now prosper.

However, there are certain particular considerations which must be actively brought into play, to enable the realization of such goals as I have specified, heretofore, in a competent vision of the present and future times, as now follows, here, immediately, next.

Vernadsky's Unique Principle of Mankind

As I had indicated, in this present report, earlier, the realization of the goals which I have identified here, this far, depends upon an urgent need for systemic revision of the heretofore present notion of the specific practical role of mankind within the Solar system itself, as such. That is to emphasize, that the heretofore accepted notions of mankind's efficient place within both the Solar systemic system, and beyond, must be radically rectified, and that strictly according to the particular standard stipulated by V.I. Vernadsky. Mankind must now be recognized as the supreme power operating within the process of development of mankind's policies of practice respecting relations within and of the Solar system as a whole: that as Vernadsky had strictly emphasized while he had been still living.

We must now recognize, that space and time no longer exist of themselves as reliable notions, nor with actually practical efficiency for mankind; only the role

National Optical Astronomy Observatories

"The metric of evolution in the Solar System itself, is not merely life-forms, but, only, as known this far, the self-evolution of the human will unique to the human species' own principle of a universal chemistry, the increase of the energy-flux density enabling the progressive evolution upward of mankind itself...." Shown: the Milky Way Galaxy.

assigned to mankind by our given nature, has useful merit, precisely as V.I. Vernadsky has made that point. Mankind itself, is the only proper determinant of the practical meaning of what is, mistakenly called a basis based upon a mistaken notion of an actual combination of time, space, and matter, presently popularly presumed to be available to humanity's will. The actual basis is only the creative (i.e., noëtic) powers attributable to the individual human mind, expressed through increase of the power of the human species to change the course of development of the life of the human species within (immediately) the Solar system as such: Vernadsky's most essential expression of the identifiably essential principle of the existence of our human species.

A Universal Principle:

The metric of evolution in the Solar system itself, is not merely life-forms-in-general; but, only, as known this far, the self-evolution of the human will unique to the human species' own principle of a universal chemistry, the principled increase of the energy-flux density enabling the progressive evolution upward of mankind itself: the evolution of mankind which prompts the in-

creased power expressed as higher characteristic evolutions upward by the societies of the human species, into constant rises in the power of mankind's self-existence and effective revolutionary progresses in mankind's appropriate authority for the evolution of the Solar systemic system as a whole, immediately. My words, in my time, but his (Vernadsky's) explicitly stated intention.

By wielding the upward evolution of both the preconditions and evolutions of the effective power, per capita, in coordination with a rise in the living human progress to higher potencies of energy-flux densities through the means of what we name as upward-evolving chemistry as mankind's characteristic abilities, mankind daily resets the clock of the Solar system's future, as done through the means and requirements for great leaps in the applicable energy-flux density of each nation, each people, and each willing person, whose effective role must be leaps in the power of mankind within the universe, *per capita*. That is the expression of true human nature to be known: which reflects the leading revolutionary achievements of the magnificent poet of human reason, the late V.I. Vernadsky, and of principled scientific will.